Haruki Murakami's
The Wind-up Bird Chronicle

CONTINUUM CONTEMPORARIES

Also available in this series:

Forthcoming in this series:

· **HARUKI MURAKAMI'S**

The Wind-up Bird Chronicle

A READER'S GUIDE

MATTHEW STRECHER

CONTINUUM | NEW YORK | LONDON

2006

The Continuum International Publishing Group Inc
80 Maiden Lane, New York, NY 10038

The Continuum International Publishing Group Ltd
The Tower Building, 11 York Road, London SE1 7NX

www.continuumbooks.com

Copyright © 2002 by Matthew Strecher

Printed in the United States of America

Library of Congress Cataloging-in-Publication Data

Strecher, Matthew.
    Haruki Murakami's The wind-up bird chronicle : a reader's guide /
Matthew Strecher.
        p. cm. — (Continuum contemporaries)
    Includes bibliographical references.
    ISBN 0-8264-5239-6 (alk. paper)
    1. Murakami, Haruki, 1949- . Nejimaki-dori kuronikuru.   I.
Title. II. Series.
    PL856.U673 N4538 2002
    895.6'35—dc21   2001047381

Contents

Acknowledgments

The process of writing this book was aided by a number of people. In particular I would like to thank Jay Rubin for providing me with important insights relating to the translation of *The Wind-up Bird Chronicle*, and to Haruki Murakami, who provided publication and sales information, as well as details concerning his life and experiences both before and during his career as a novelist. I also extend gratitude to my colleagues at Tōyō University for their encouragement and support, and to David Barker at Continuum Publishers for his seemingly endless patience. Finally, I would like to thank my wife, Mei, and my children, Victor and Elizabeth, for cheerfully putting up with my frequent absences from home to work on this.

for Victor and Barbara Strecher
and
Li Tzu-Yin and Huang Qing-Liang

1

The Novelist

THE CHANGING FACE OF JAPANESE LITERATURE

In 1979, nearing his thirtieth birthday, a jazz café owner named Haruki Murakami surprised himself, his friends, and especially Japanese literary critics by winning the Gunzo Prize for New Writers with his début novel, *Hear the Wind Sing*. From this point Murakami's fiction, along with that of other young writers seemingly intent on resisting the more seriously artistic paradigms of the Japanese novel, began subtly but inexorably to undermine some of the most basic aspects of the distinction between "serious" and "popular" writing. It became increasingly difficult to separate serious, artistic, socially critical works ("literature") from merely entertaining ones ("fiction"). Literary "art" began to give way to the art of "storytelling."

Murakami's own contribution to this effort has been described in a variety of expressions: some Japanese critics have argued that the author's appeal lay in his "Americanization" of Japanese writing, that the Japanese literary language itself changed as a result of the author's innovations. There is something to this. The author's taste in literature and his prose style were formed early on by a steady diet of American paperback fiction—Truman Capote, Raymond Chandler, Kurt Vonnegut, Raymond Carver, John Irving, and so forth. Indeed, part of the simplicity that has come to be so much a Murakami trademark is attributable (if the author himself is to be believed) to his early practice of writing in English, then translating himself back into Japanese. In so doing, he developed a style that would have made any minimalist proud.

But Murakami's style is not just simple; it is direct. Absent is much of the mysterious ambiguity that has come to be associated with other Japanese authors who have come to be known outside of Japan, such as Yasunari Kawabata, Yukio Mishima, and Jun'ichiro Tanizaki. For this reason there is an uncommonly "un-Japanese" flavor to Murakami's use of the Japanese language, leading fellow novelist and Nobel laureate Kenzaburo Oe to comment that "Murakami writes in Japanese, but his writing isn't really Japanese. If you translate it into American English it can be read very naturally in New York" (*Japan in the World*, 172). German critic Jürgen Stalph noted similarly only a few years ago that foreign readers—German readers in his case—found Murakami accessible and thrilling because of the seamlessness with which his Japanese seems to be translatable into other languages (*Kokubungaku*, 104–108).

This has led some critics to speculate that the latest generation of Japanese writers is antagonistic to the entrenched "old guard" of Japanese literature, and to a point they are right. Murakami, however, denies that he has intentionally pitted himself against the Bundan, Japan's literary guild, the formal establishment that decides what is of value and what is not in Japanese writing. "I didn't write in order to resist the Bundan," says Murakami of *Hear the Wind Sing*; "I could never have exerted myself so much for that. I just wrote what I wanted, the way I wanted" (Kawamoto, *Bungakukai*,

39). Nevertheless, Murakami and others like him represent a challenge to the old guard of Japanese literature, a new voice that engages the ambiguities of the present age, the looming questions of the new century.

Of course, resistance of this kind is nothing new in Japanese literature. Indeed, since the end of the World War II Japanese writers have sought to redefine their role in their society, assuming a more political, socially responsible stance. Having failed, with few exceptions, to form an intellectual voice of resistance to militarism in the years from 1930 to 1945, many of the younger writers of the postwar made it their mission to foster social and political awareness and responsibility among their readership. While some aesthetes—notably Kawabata and Mishima—continued to assert the primacy of art in their writing, others—Oe, Makoto Oda, Takeshi Kaiko—used their writing as an avenue through which to denounce the Vietnam War, nuclear weapons, and Japan's inability to produce a coherent foreign policy independent of Washington. Such writing fit in well with the spirit of 1960s counterculture in Japan, the principal targets of which were the Vietnam War, nuclear proliferation, the continued U.S. military presence in Japan (especially Okinawa), and Japan's alliance with NATO against the Warsaw Pact. Writers who tackled these issues were, needless to say, seen as the cutting edge of their own literary era, as spokesmen for counterculture and a new generation in general, much as Norman Mailer, Joseph Heller and Truman Capote were read in the United States.

Among their principal readership were young people like Murakami, just reaching college age in the final years of the 1960s. Murakami himself entered Tokyo's Waseda University in 1968, having left his hometown of Ashiya, an affluent suburb of Kobe, for the first time. Concerning this move to Tokyo Murakami clearly had mixed feelings, for a variety of reasons: Kobe is part of the Kansai district, a traditional rival (both culturally and, in medieval days, militarily) of the Kanto region of which Tokyo is the center; he had never been away from home before; his friends were all in the Kobe area, and even his sweetheart lived there at the time. Nevertheless he left all this behind, simply because he felt it was time to leave his past behind and do something completely new. In his own words, "I just wanted to be somebody else. I was stuck in one place. Many people, many of my friends stayed in Kansai, but I couldn't. I needed action." (Interview with Murakami) One senses in this a desire to rebel against the man he was at the time, to make a sudden, radical change in aspect.

This kind of rebellious spirit is not unusual for Murakami, who has quietly found ways to be different since childhood. As the only child of not one but two teachers of Japanese language arts, one might have expected Murakami to be naturally drawn to literature, but for precisely this reason the author deliberately steered himself away from the Japanese "classics." This is not to say that he ignored them altogether, however; even Murakami admits that he read the "greats" at one time or another—Soseki Natsume, Tanizaki, Kawabata, and so forth. He is also reasonably well-read in Japan's premodern literature, and claims Akinari Ueda, a mid-eighteenth century writer of supernatural tales, as one of his favorite writers of all time.

But in general Murakami's guiding principle in life has been an urge to be different, not an easy aspiration in Japan. His ideas about literature, both how to read it and how to write it, came not from the Japanese public school curriculum, but from his own fascination with American paperback literature, an interest that bloomed for him during his teenage years. It delighted him to learn that he could, with some persistence, read books in a foreign language, and this may account in part for the international flair of his writing style today. Above all, though, the appeal of such reading was the fact that few others were doing it at the same time. In a similar way, while others studied English as part of their standard curriculum, Murakami learned the language through his reading of such popular literature.

His urge to rebellion took on new and interesting directions in the late 1960s. While so many other students in Japan — particularly at Waseda — were demonstrating against the conservative right, Murakami elected to go his own way. He rarely joined the demonstrations, and when he did, he asserts, it was not as part of them, but in his own right. This is not to say that he was opposed to the basic goals of the demonstrators; only that he found them too predictable, too hung up on the ideas of others. "I was a loner," he says, "so I didn't belong to any political organizations or anything. I hated that. I hated to be with other people. I just wanted to be myself. But if you wanted to be yourself, you couldn't really be 'political' " (Interview with Murakami)

His scorn for the student left as well as the conservative right is especially clear in his 1987 bestselling novel *Norwegian Wood*, in which he describes the takeover of a classroom by a helmeted pair of student activists. The two proceed to pass out handbills demanding that the present form of university be dismantled, then make a speech that bores the students almost as much as their professor had done before. This seems to reflect Murakami's own impressions of the common run of student radicals he encountered between 1968–1969.

Some were true radicals, but most of them were just assholes. I couldn't stand them. They had no imagination. Like, some of these guys were Marxists. I had nothing against Marxism at the time, but these guys weren't really speaking their own words. They just talked in slogans all the time, excerpts from books, that sort of thing. I mean, the words they used were strong and beautiful, but they weren't their own. (Interview with Murakami)

Murakami, then, rejected not the causes of the demonstrations, but the means used to get there. Much later he would agree with psychologist Kawai Hayao's exasperated declaration that Japanese student radicals, while claiming to be offering a new way of thinking, were in fact merely reinventing the conventional, for when they rebelled, they did so in groups, taking care that their actions always conformed to those of their fellow radicals.

DARKNESS AND LIGHT

Murakami Haruki himself acknowledges that there was little out of the ordinary in his childhood, save for the fact that he was an only child, something that seems to have had an impact on his writing, especially in the intensely lonely nature of his characters. He was born in Kyoto in January of 1949, and moved to Ashiya when he was three years old. Ashiya, then as now, was an area inhabited mainly by upwardly mobile types; Murakami refers to it as a "yuppie" district. This, too, appears in his stories, usually as a reaction against the wealthy affectations of the people who live there. One of the more colorful figures in *Hear the Wind Sing*, a rebellious hippie known as "Rat," comes from this area and background, and the first words out of his mouth in that work are, "The rich can all go eat shit." In a short story from around the same time entitled "The Seashore in May" (1981), the protagonist sits on the beach looking up at the affluent skyline of Ashiya and wishes aloud that "all those buildings would just collapse into a pile of rubble."

But in general, Murakami insists that his childhood was ordinary. He had friends, he lived a normal childhood. Only one incident seems to have remained strong enough in his memory to emerge in his fiction as well: at approximately the age of three, Murakami fell into a drainage ditch and, prior to his rescue, faced the terrifying darkness of an underground culvert. This memory reemerges vividly in *The Wind-up Bird Chronicle* as one character's earliest memory:

"I can still picture everything that happened. I'm lying on my back and being swept along by the water. The sides of the stream tower over me like high stone walls, and overhead is the blue sky. Sharp, clear blue. I'm being swept along in the flow. Swish, swish, faster and faster. But I can't understand what it means. And then all of a sudden I *do* understand — that there's darkness lying ahead. *Real* darkness. Soon it comes and tries to drink me down. I can feel a cold shadow beginning to wrap itself around me. That's my earliest memory." (p. 105)

The author himself insists that this has had no lasting psychological impact on him as a person, but the darkness of that underground waterway has manifested itself in his writing in a variety of ways, chiefly as a fundamental dichotomy between the world of light above ground, and a world of darkness beneath it. This gloomy realm has taken on many forms in the author's writing from the beginning: the underworld (in the Orphean sense); the world beneath the ground (subways, wells, etc.); the vastness of outer space; and, of course, the unconscious. Murakami himself describes this as a manifestation of *yin* and *yang*, opposite, yet mutually necessary complementary forces:

I have always been attracted by *yin* and *yang*, and by mythology in general. It's a popular pattern: two worlds, one bright, one dark. You find the same kind of stories in the Western world. And of course, if you read Japan's *Kojiki* (Record of Ancient Matters; ca. 712 C.E.), you find the story of Izanagi and Izanami. Izanagi's wife dies, and lives in the "underworld." Izanagi enters the world of the dead to see her. The story of Orpheus is the same. The big difference in Japanese mythology is that you can go underground very easily if you want to. In Greek myths you have to go through all kinds of trials first. (Interview with Murakami)

The darkness, for Murakami, is always the place where the unconscious mind reigns supreme, where the conscious visitor feels unnerved, even unwelcome, and wrestles with an alterego, an inner self struggling with the outer consciousness for dominance over the whole identity.

MURAKAMI AND LONERISM

Yet another recurring point in Murakami literature seems to be its quiet, ordinary, yet intensely lonely protagonist. This, too, is a reflection of the author's own preference for being left alone, something manifested in his lifestyle choices. His penchant for reading comes at least to some extent from a natural disposition to be antisocial. His peculiar attitude toward the student demonstrations during the 1960s is also related to this. He has admitted an early interest in becoming a screenwriter during his college years, but elected not to follow it through because he couldn't bear the thought that to transform the script into film would require him to work with others. Obviously, Murakami prefers not to be a team player, and neither do his protagonists.

This tendency toward lonerism turns up in his stories in a variety of ways. For years Murakami wrote from the perspective of an unobtrusive first-person narrator calling himself only "Boku," an informal version of the first-person singular pronoun. The effect of this has been to lend his stories an intimacy, creating a sense of closeness, or at least familiarity, between narrator and reader. At the same time, we can never really escape the loneliness of the Murakami protagonist, who seems always to be dealing with the loss of friends, loved ones, his youth, and so forth. Readers of *A Wild Sheep Chase* (1989), the author's first release in the English-speaking world, will remember this sense of loss in the protagonist's quest for his best friend, Rat, who has actually been missing since the end of *Hear the Wind Sing*. This loneliness intensifies as the protagonist loses his girlfriend and must pass several solitary days at Rat's isolated villa deep in the mountains of Hokkaido.

Since emerging on the Japanese literary scene, the author himself has gone to impressive lengths over the years to maintain a reasonable wall of privacy for himself. As much as Murakami limited his social intercourse to a small circle of friends during his college years, and even during the years from 1973 to 1983 or so when he owned and operated a jazz cafe in Tokyo called "Peter Cat," he has redoubled his efforts to keep himself at arm's length since achieving real stardom as a writer in the mid-1980s. Finding it difficult to work amid the many demands of living in Japan, he left Tokyo in 1987, traveling in Italy and Greece for three years, and followed this with four years on the east coast of the United States. He is very candid about his motivations for living abroad: "Japanese do not have any agents. Too many people would call, ask for me. My wife would say, 'He is busy.' But that embarrasses male callers. I had to respond" (Wright, *Boston Magazine*).

Fortunately for Murakami, by 1994 he had made enough money from the sale of more than two million two-volume sets of his 1987 bestseller *Norwegian Wood* (released in English in September of 2000) to buy himself a little privacy. By maintaining several residences in Tokyo and allowing himself to leave the country whenever necessary, he has managed to avoid some of these unwanted distractions. "Fortunately," says Murakami, "when you make a lot of money you can buy things like time and freedom, and that's a great thing. I don't care about fashionable cars or a big house. I never wanted that. I just wanted a little freedom." (Interview with Murakami) This notwithstanding, Murakami today lives in one of Tokyo's most notoriously high-rent districts, and reportedly drives a Ferrari!

THE POWER OF THE STORY

For Murakami Haruki, nothing supercedes the importance of telling the story, a fact that is entirely consistent with his rejection of the student movements of the 1960s, his (intentional or not) resistance to the Bundan, and indeed his general dislike of literary criticism. (Murakami does not read critical writing on his own work, preferring instead to heed the comments of his wife.) As noted above, he claims never to have willfully "resisted" the paradigms of "pure" literature; it has simply turned out that way. Nonetheless, he is not without his own views on the purpose of fiction, and much of his thinking differs from more traditional views on the subject.

As a useful example, Japan's most recent literary Nobel laureate, Kenzaburo Oe, has insisted repeatedly that the true purpose of literature should be to produce a working model for the next generation of intellectuals to challenge. "The purpose of literature — insofar as man is obviously a historical being — is to create a model of a contemporary age which envelops past and future and a human model that lives in that age," writes Oe (1989, p. 193). The notion of "enveloping past and future" refers to the modern intellectual's responsibility to engage past systems of thought, create new ones that address these systems, and to recognize the need for future generations to do the same. It is, in short, a way of understanding history as a living, unresolvable debate that leads, inevitably, to more highly evolved systems of thought.

But Murakami insists that such an atmosphere of "challenge" and "opposition" with regard to intellectual systems of thought simply does not exist in contemporary Japan. Such concepts are out of date, having collapsed with the fall of the Soviet Union and the reunification of East and West Berlin. The era of the Bundan and "pure" literature peaked, and then declined, in the 1950s and 1960s. "It was convenient in those days to think of pure literature and mass literature as completely different from one another. But since the 1970s things have changed. Communism has faded away, and the world is collapsing" (interview with Murakami). Literature is collapsing, too, he says, and with it the basic principle that the role of the fiction writer must be to illustrate transcendent truths. Instead, he believes in the power of stories, of words themselves, to allow readers to develop their own personal sense of truth and reality, and to make sense of the world for themselves.

Murakami also rejects the notion of literature as Art, and the emphasis on intellectualism that characterized the celebrated literary figures of the 1960s, including Oe. It would be a mistake, however, to imagine that he feels no sense of responsibility as a writer. Rather, his responsibility lies in meeting the new challenge that all writers face: in producing stories that impress readers sufficiently to make them look at their own lives, and apply what they take from the pages of the story to their own experiences, not on the intellectual level but on a deeply empathetic, emotional one. Offering a tongue-in-cheek example, Murakami puts it this way:

In *Norwegian Wood* there is a place where Midori asks the protagonist, "How much do you love me?" And he has to make up a story. If he just says, "I love you very, very much," she will never be impressed. So he has to make up a story. Like, "I was walking in the woods in springtime, and a bear came along, and. . . ." Just like that. Then she's impressed. That scenery, that dialogue, that feeling . . . everything there expresses how he loves her. *That's* the power of the story. Pure literature never has that kind of power; it's just words. You could never seduce anyone with it! (Interview with Murakami)

More serious examples of his commitment as a writer to impressing his readers with their own sense of responsibility are plentiful. While his fiction in the 1980s was admittedly self-absorbed — reflective mostly of Murakami's need to understand why the commitment to ideals that defined his generation in the 1960s faded — his writing in the last ten years or so is more outwardly directed, more activist. Beginning, by some accounts, with his 1992 novel *South of the Border, West of the Sun* (translated by Philip Gabriel), Murakami's lonely protagonist began to look outward, to seek deeper and more intense relationships with other people.

The path to establishing these relationships lies in the power of the story. Murakami's protagonists place a great deal of emphasis on listening to the stories of others. It is an element that appears prominently in his second book, *Pinball 1973* (1980), in which the protagonist recounts the stories told to him by his girlfriend, who is now dead. Whereas in his early works these stories serve the purpose of helping the protagonist achieve self-awareness, however, in more recent works Murakami channels them into the protagonist's efforts to achieve mutual understanding with others. This is the source of frustration in *South of the Border, West of the Sun*, for the protagonist's failure to "connect" with the one woman he truly loves is directly related to the fact that she never reveals anything about herself to him.

This is also a central theme in Murakami's most recent works. In *The Sputnik Sweetheart*, for instance, the heroine, a sensitive young writer named Sumire, disappears, leaving no clues to her whereabouts except for a laptop computer and a single floppy disk. By reading the stories Sumire has left behind on the disk, the protagonist is able to piece together something of what has happened to her, and we even have a plausible, if somewhat metaphysical, solution to her present whereabouts.

Murakami carries this emphasis on storytelling into his nonfiction works as well, most notably in his 1997 *Underground*, a collection of interviews with survivors of the 1995 sarin gas incident, in which members of the AUM Shinrikyo cult released toxic sarin gas in several major Tokyo subway stations. Murakami's decision to interview the victims of the incident emerged primarily from his belief that these victims had not been given a chance to tell their stories, unlike the cult members, whose lives and stories had been reported in great detail by the mass media. "I had been frustrated by the few reports on victims, in sharp contrast to the flood of information about the AUM Shinrikyo . . . I felt I had to find out the other side of the story" (Rau and Murakami, *Asiaweek*). He went on to say that "I am genuinely interested in people and their stories. I enjoyed talking to every one of [the victims]" (ibid.).

In *The Wind-up Bird Chronicle*, as we shall find shortly, personal narratives are a crucial part of the novel's structure. Through the many narratives told from varying perspectives to the work's protagonist, Toru Okada, complex relationships are established between the characters of the novel, as well as links between events of the distant past and the present. All of these narratives, finally, serve a single end: to help the characters discover their identities, their individual roles in the events of the contemporary world Murakami creates.

2

The Novel

INTRODUCTION

The *Wind-up Bird Chronicle* is, to date, the most focused, and at the same time the most complex work of fiction yet produced by Haruki Murakami. Not only is the narrative a mixture of the magical and the realistic, of distinct historical periods, of a sometimes bewildering pastiche of narrative voices; strictly speaking the novel is not even a single, unified narrative, but a combination of at least three major narratives, all of which are connected with one another by the enigmatic presence of the "wind-up bird."

The "main" narrative of *The Wind-up Bird Chronicle* is, by virtue of its persistence from the beginning to the end of the story, the quest of Toru to understand, and finally, to recover his wife, Kumiko, from a peculiar kind of entrapment. It is peculiar because he must free her from the fetters of her own inner self, for she has been overcome by an inner force that lies within her unconscious self. This leads Toru into inevitable conflict with her brother, Noboru Wataya, who begins the work as an academic and a charlatan intellectual, but whose career as the leading young politician of the day develops with the narrative.

Toru's conflict with Kumiko and Noboru lies hidden deep within the history of the relationship between those two characters, something Toru fails to recognize until it is too late. Noboru is revealed fairly early on as a sinister character and Toru has no difficulty in recognizing him as a figure representing danger to himself and his wife. What he does not understand — and perhaps there is no way he could — is that Noboru's sinister side is born of an "evil nature" he carries within his blood. More importantly, Kumiko shares this dark, inner nature herself.

The critical failure of Toru to understand this about his wife, or indeed, much of anything else, is the root cause of their problems as a couple. Toru is able, at the very least, to sense that there is something mysterious about Kumiko fairly early in the story, but he clearly has no idea how deep the problem lies, nor how truly alienated he really is from his wife. Following a seemingly minor argument that arises from Toru's preparation of green peppers and beef, a culinary combination that Kumiko cannot abide, she accuses Toru of being too wrapped up in himself to notice anything about her at all. Reflecting on the incident, Toru begins to wonder how much he really *does* understand about Kumiko.

I had lived with her all this time, unaware how much she hated these things. In themselves they were trivial. Stupid. Something to laugh off, not make a big issue out of. We'd had a little tiff and would have forgotten about it in a couple of days.

But this was different. It was bothering me in a strange new way, digging at me like a little fish bone caught in the throat. Maybe — just maybe — it was more crucial than it had seemed. Maybe this was it: the fatal blow. Or maybe it was just the beginning of what would be the fatal blow. (30)

Toru, of course, has no idea at this point how right he is in imagining that this is the beginning of a much more serious conflict, one that will lead, ultimately, to the destruction either of Noboru Wataya or himself.

Book One of the novel ("The Thieving Magpie") begins with the search for the couple's missing cat, named (as a joke) "Noboru Wataya." This in itself hints at the direction the story will take, as the quest for Noboru Wataya the cat masks the more critical quest Toru will undertake, not only for his wife, who disappears at the beginning of Book Two ("Bird as Prophet"), but for the real Noboru Wataya, who gradually emerges as Toru's arch enemy and alter ego.

This is not a new theme for Murakami. The hero of A *Wild Sheep Chase*, for instance, a nameless public relations man, is sent off on a similar quest for a quasi-mythical sheep thought to bestow other-worldly powers on anyone fortunate (or unfortunate!) enough to become its host. In the course of this quest, the hero also seeks his best friend (and alter ego), known as Rat. In that book, too, the hero is unaware that his search for the one is simultaneously a quest for the other, until he finds both sheep and Rat at the same place.

MAY KASAHARA: NAIVE ORACLE

Murakami heroes rarely undertake these quests without help; in A *Wild Sheep Chase* the hero is guided by a clairvoyant girlfriend who uses her psychic abilities to lead him to precisely the right locations, speeding the narrative along considerably. He is also aided by a bizarre character called the Sheepman—more of a psychotic episode than a character—of whom I will write more below. In the sequel to that work, *Dance Dance Dance*, the same hero searches for the girlfriend (who disappears near the end of A *Wild Sheep Chase*), as well as his lost idealism, with the help of a clairvoyant teenage girl named Yuki, and the Sheepman, who also returns from that story.

In *The Wind-up Bird Chronicle*, Toru has help from a variety of psychics—the enigmatic Kano sisters, Malta and Creta, and old Mr. Honda—and from others who simply fill in the historical details for him. But no one seems to have the answers he really needs, or the temerity to "tell it like it is," more than May Kasahara, a sixteen year-old high school dropout who lives in Toru's neighborhood.

May Kasahara performs a central, even critical role in this story by expressing directly much of what we, the reader, might wish Toru would understand on his own. As a person, she is not much to look at; a skinny, awkward-looking girl in sunglasses and shorts, nearly always smoking one of her "Hope regulars," a popular brand of cigarette in Japan. But she is astute, and somehow manages always to put her finger exactly on the source of Toru's problems. Her naturally candid nature allows her to tell Toru the truth about himself. It is she who wonders how Toru can know so little about his wife, despite having lived together for six years (190), and who asks the really tough questions, like whether he would take Kumiko back if she had been sleeping with someone else (196).

In a technical sense, May Kasahara also allows us to see Toru's moral superiority, in contrast with the darkly sexual nature of Noboru Wataya. There is always a sexual tension between May Kasahara and Toru, expressed more by her than him. She often touches him, gently strokes him, making him keenly aware of her body. She talks freely with him about the size of her breasts, and dresses in ways that reveal her girlish, yet obviously female, body to him. When he is tired, she has him lie quietly while she caresses his hand, or kisses his flushed cheeks. In one of her letters, she even expresses (or almost expresses) her willingness to be raped by him.

But Toru's inner nature, one of forbearance and self-control, will not allow him to betray the trust that May Kasahara shows in him by committing what would be, for him, an unpardonably immoral act. This, too, is something that has occurred before in Murakami's writing: the hero of *Hard-Boiled Wonderland and the End of the World*, for instance, is propositioned suggestively by a sexy seventeen-year-old who clearly wants him to provide her first sexual experience, but he defers. The protagonist of *Dance Dance Dance* similarly will not respond to the infatuation of a teenage girl for whom he is temporarily responsible. The purpose of these relationships is always to demonstrate the control with which Murakami's heroes handle their sexual drives, not to suggest that sexuality is bad, but that there is "good" sexuality and "bad" sexuality, and the morally superior character knows the difference. This, as we shall see, contrasts with the behavior of Noboru Wataya, for whom sexuality is a means to power and control.

SEXUALITY AND THE "OTHER"

Sexuality *does* play a role in Toru's life, however, and it has greater importance to him than he is willing to admit. The novel begins, in fact, with Toru receiving telephone calls from a woman whose voice he does not recognize, who begs him for "ten minutes" of his time so that they might "understand one another." He finds it exceedingly strange that she knows so much about him—his exact age, the fact that he is out of work—and yet he has no clue as to who she might be. When she calls again later her talk is unmistakably sexual, and he prudishly hangs up on her.

Early on we suspect a connection between this woman, pleading for mutual understanding with Toru, and his self-admission that he knows nothing about his wife. In fact, the "telephone woman" *is* Kumiko, but she is not the same woman Toru knows; this Kumiko is sexually charged, driven by uncontrolled (and uncontrollable) passion. It is not possible for Toru to recognize this, however, for this unconscious manifestation of Kumiko expresses her desire in terms so direct that Toru cannot associate them with his self-controlled wife. Thus he misses his early chances to "discover" Kumiko and save his relationship with her.

Sexuality also plays a key role in Toru's relationship with the Kano sisters, Malta and Creta. Malta Kano, a clairvoyant brought in by Kumiko to help locate their missing cat, is assisted by her sister, Creta, whose connection with Toru is that she just happens to have been sexually assaulted by Noboru Wataya, causing some kind of "defilement" that has displaced her "self," forcing her to construct a new identity for herself. This in turn leads Creta Kano to pursue a sexual relationship with Toru, in order to help reverse the damage done by Noboru. Appearing in his dreams on two separate occasions while he naps, she has sex with him, causing him to ejaculate. At the time Toru believes he has simply had erotic dreams that spilled over (literally) into the waking world, but when Creta visits him in reality she is able to describe the scenes in detail, making it clear that they really happened, but in a different realm of consciousness. " 'Of course, we did not have relations in reality. When you ejaculated, it was not into me, physically, but in your own consciousness. Do you see? It was a fabricated consciousness. Still, the two of us share the consciousness of having had relations with each other' " (214). This is possible, she explains, because she is a "prostitute of the mind," able to join her mind sexually with those of others. Later she explains that she is "able to divide myself into a physical self and a nonphysical self" (308), and thus to move some mental aspect of herself—her mind, her soul, her consciousness—to another place.

Toru learns much from this experience with Creta. He is intrigued by the fact that in their second unconscious meeting she not only wore one of Kumiko's dresses, but even seemed to turn into Kumiko during their intercourse. This gives him the idea that the key to finding Kumiko may lie in developing the same ability that Creta uses to enter his own unconscious realm more or less at will. After hearing Mamiya's story about a near-vision at the bottom of his well in Mongolia, and having been told that there is a dry well in the yard of a nearby house by May Kasahara, Toru decides that the well is the gateway to his inner self, and this is where he goes to pursue his quest.

THE WELL AND THE MARK

The dreamscape in which this part of the story takes place is a vast, labyrinthine hotel (mirroring the chaos of the unconscious), the core of which for Toru is Room 208. There, he re-encounters the seductive "telephone woman"—and sometimes Creta herself—and shares the details of his quest with her. More importantly, however, he is not permitted to *see* her—the room is shrouded in darkness—but can only hear her voice. Her voice, however, remains unfamiliar to him.

Clearly, this unconscious hotel is the key to solving the mystery of Kumiko's disappearance, a fact that Toru himself comes to understand by the middle of the novel. At the same time, it is also a realm of danger, hiding unknown enemies who seek to harm Toru for reasons he cannot yet fathom. He learns this during one of his "visits" when the door to Room 208 suddenly opens, and a shadowy figure enters with something that gleams like the blade of a knife. Frantically he makes his escape through the wall, but not before the "telephone woman" joins herself to him in a different way:

I felt the woman's tongue coming into my mouth. Warm and soft, it probed every crevice and it wound around my own tongue. The heavy smell of flower petals stroked the walls of my lungs. Down in my loins, I felt a dull need to come. Clamping my eyes closed, I fought it. A moment later, I felt a kind of intense heat on my right cheek. It was an odd sensation. I felt no pain, only the awareness that there was heat there. I couldn't tell whether the heat was coming from the outside or boiling up inside me. (249)

What has happened here may be as unclear to us as it is to Toru initially, but after emerging from several days in the well he returns home and shaves off his beard, upon which he discovers a dark purple mark on his right cheek, "about the size of an infant's palm" (288). He, of course, has no idea what the mark signifies, but cannot help noticing as time goes on that it is warm, and seems to be alive. "Perhaps the mark was a brand that had been impressed on me by that strange dream or illusion or whatever it was," he tells himself. *"That was no dream,* they were telling me through the mark: *It really happened. And every time you look in the mirror now, you will be forced to remember it"* (289).

But there is much more to the mark than just this. It signifies yet another kind of joining, through which the "telephone woman" has placed *something* inside of him. The mark is a new, embryonic consciousness, one that will live and grow in his cheek until it is "born" coincident with the completion of his quest. In short, the mark may be read as yet another manifestation of Kumiko herself, providing a living, real-world link to the unconscious realm in which she lies trapped. Like other such manifestations, it will disappear only when it is no longer needed, the point when Toru defeats his enemy.

The means to achieving this end will be the final showdown between Toru and Noboru, and the quest for Kumiko/Noboru will thus conclude in a deadly battle between basic elements—good and evil—that is grounded in violence and sexuality, forcing Toru to decide how far he is willing to go in order to rescue Kumiko from the bonds that hold her. At the same time, as he does in receiving the woman's tongue into his mouth, he will discover a kind of "passive" sexuality that proves *liberating* to those with whom he comes into contact, as a means of recovering their own sense of active selfhood.

NARRATIVE TWO: THE "FORGOTTEN" WAR

Violence is also an integral part of the second major narrative in *The Wind-up Bird Chronicle*, one that takes place long before Toru is born. This is the story told to Toru, both face to face and through correspondence, by Mr. Honda, an ex-soldier with clairvoyant powers, and Lieutenant Mamiya, who fought alongside Honda in the "forgotten" war at Nomonhan in 1939.

The real purpose behind the portions of the narrative that deal with World War II is to reveal an ancestry to the present conflict between Toru and Noboru, and in this regard it is successful. Its principal characters are Honda, who plays a role in Mamiya's fate; Mamiya himself, a man who, like Toru, seems to display a basic sense of decency amidst the indecency of war; and "Boris the Manskinner," a cold, sadistic monster who seems counterpoised to Mamiya in much the same way that Noboru comes to be positioned opposite Toru in the modern era.

Mamiya's narrative is a horrifying one, to say the least, and represents a new level of graphic violence in Murakami fiction. His story begins with his being sent on a top-secret mission into Soviet-controlled Outer Mongolia with Honda (from Toru's narrative), an intelligence officer named Yamamoto, and a foot soldier named Hamano. There, with the exception of Honda, who escapes, they are captured by a Mongolian patrol. Soon afterward a Soviet intelligence officer arrives whose nickname, "Boris the Manskinner," proves to be gruesomely apt. Finding Yamamoto unwilling to talk, he has him staked to the ground, then orders him skinned alive.

He fails, however, to learn what he needs to know, and gives up the pursuit. As a compensatory gesture, he grants Mamiya a small chance of survival, ordering him to be taken out into the desert and dropped into a deep well. There, Mamiya experiences an epiphany of sorts, borne on the brief entry of sunlight into his darkened prison, but he fails to grasp its meaning before it disappears. Feeling he has missed his sole chance to understand the meaning of his life, he despairs and awaits death.

Mamiya, however, is not destined to die on the Asian continent, as he has already been told previously by the clairvoyant Honda. Thus, it comes as no great surprise when he is rescued — by Honda — and brought back to his own lines.

His ordeal, however, is not over. In a much later narrative, passed on to Toru in a long letter, Mamiya relates how he managed to survive the massed attack of a Soviet armored division in the final days of the war, and found himself, minus one hand, alive in a Soviet labor camp after the war. There, again, he meets Boris the Manskinner, who starts out a fellow inmate but will shortly take over control of the camp. In time Mamiya gains Boris' confidence, hoping for a chance to take revenge on him. Unfortunately for Mamiya, however, he cannot kill Boris. Even given two easy opportunities to blow his enemy's head off at pointblank range, he is unable to do so. Eventually he returns to Japan, bearing Boris' final curse on him: " 'Wherever you may be, you can never be happy. You will never love anyone or be loved by anyone. That is my curse. I will not kill you. But I do not spare you out of goodwill. I have killed many people over the years, and I will go on to kill many more. But I never kill anyone whom there is no need to kill' " (567). And true to this prophesy, Mamiya lives out the rest of his days in quiet misery, an "empty shell" of a man.

The purpose of Mamiya's narrative, I think, is to provide a historical pattern, a narrative ancestor, to the situation in which Toru finds himself in the present. The relationships established here are of critical importance: Mamiya, a force of good, opposes Boris, the embodiment of evil. Two worlds collide, one of controlled gentility and forbearance—something also displayed by Toru, as noted above—the other one of pure malevolence and ambition. In that struggle between elemental forces, Mamiya loses everything; his failure to destroy this evil presence costs him his soul. Cast into archetypal terms, as I believe we must with the whole of *The Windup Bird Chronicle*, Mamiya fails to restore life to the wasteland of death (seen both in the wilds of the Mongolian desert and the labor camp in barren Siberia) that remained following World War II.

But there is another, equally important, subnarrative to the saga of Mamiya in the war, and this is the tension that is established between the will of the individual and the power of the State. Murakami himself is primarily interested in this aspect of the war as part of his project of recovering the individual voices of those who were involved. Indeed, the same impulse that led the author to seek the fuller story of the sarin gas incident, including the first-hand views of the cult members themselves, leads him to wonder what role government plays—especially a strict, militaristic one such as ruled Japan at that time—in the atrocities committed during war. "It is the same with the Rape of Nanking," Murakami commented in 1997. "Who did it? The military or the individual soldiers? Just how responsible are individuals in a society where they relinquish their free will to the system?" (Rao and Murakami, *Asiaweek*).

Murakami does not absolve those who commit atrocities, but he does suggest the possibility of mitigating circumstances, particularly the lack of individual freedom at times of international tension. Sometimes individual evil and ambition cause suffering, as we see in the case of Boris the Manskinner, but even Boris represents not so much an individual but a system, of which he is a part. Without the Soviet system, there might be no Boris. Similarly, were there no Japanese State, there might be no war, and thus no need to carry out stupid orders that waste human life.

We see signs of dissent and hostility toward the Japanese State, whose leaders' arrogance and ambition led to disaster, in the comments of many of those involved. Hamano expresses it to Mamiya — an act in itself that could have been regarded as treason — as they sit on the wrong side of the Khalkha River in Soviet-held territory: "I'm telling you, Lieutenant, this is one war that doesn't have any Righteous Cause. It's just two sides killing each other. And the ones who get stepped on are the poor farmers, the ones without politics or ideology. . . . I can't believe that killing these people for no reason at all is going to do Japan one bit of good" (143).

This is the common soldier's perspective, one echoed later by the lieutenant put in charge of executing Chinese prisoners. But the overview, the hostility toward the politics of the war, is best and most succinctly expressed by Honda as he shows his bitterness at the aftermath of the Nomonhan disaster of 1939.

"Nomonhan was a great embarrassment for the Imperial Army, so they sent the survivors where they were most likely to be killed. The commanding officers who made such a mess of Nomonhan went on to have distinguished careers in central command. Some of the bastards even became politicians after the war. But the guys who fought their hearts out for them were almost all snuffed out." (53)

Although we are unaware of it so early in the novel, this is the first step toward establishing a link between the events of 1939–1945 (Nomonhan through the end of the war) and the events surrounding Toru and Kumiko now, for the springboard used by Noboru

Wataya to enter politics is his uncle, Yoshitaka Wataya, a member of the Diet who was at one time connected with the very members of central command who had begun the disastrous war against China. Noboru, following in these footsteps, demonstrates that the dark side of the State persists, exerting its ugly influence over the ordinary people.

Murakami's fiction has, of course, posed this sinister aspect of the Japanese State for many years—indeed, it is a central element in *A Wild Sheep Chase,* and becomes even more pronounced in *Hard-Boiled Wonderland and the End of the World.* World War II, however, is the ideal vehicle for the pursuit of this theme, for it is war, as he put it to interviewer Ian Buruma in 1996, that "stretches the tension between individuals and the state to the very limit" (*The New Yorker,* 62).

NARRATIVE THREE: CYBERSPACE AND THE UNCONSCIOUS

The third major narrative of this novel emerges entirely in Book Three ("The Birdcatcher"), and concerns the enigmatic characters Nutmeg Akasaka and her son, Cinnamon. More closely tied to the original narrative of Toru and his quest for Kumiko, this final story provides the necessary path by which the mystery of Kumiko's disappearance, the real nature of Noboru's plot, may be approached. It also offers a plausible, if puzzling, explanation of what the "wind-up bird" of the title is really supposed to be. Indeed, we might look upon Book Three as Murakami's attempt to reconnect the disparate events in Books One and Two.

Nutmeg Akasaka makes her first appearance in Book Two, but we have no more idea than Toru about who she is, or how much she will figure into the story later. Toru sits outside Shinjuku Station, watching the people go by, following his uncle's advice to sit and clear his head for a while, when a woman, well dressed and attractive, approaches him and stares at the mark on his face. She asks him if he needs anything, but when he replies in the negative, she leaves.

The woman returns in Book Three, and this time there *is* something Toru needs from her: he needs money, for he has decided to purchase the land on which the well he needs so much is located. The sum required, eighty-million yen (more than half a million U.S. dollars), is a considerable one, and it is to the evidently wealthy Nutmeg that he turns for help.

In response, she employs him in a most peculiar position for which he is uniquely qualified: Toru becomes a "healer" of sorts, a medium by which women who suffer from a mysterious unconscious imbalance restore their internal equilibrium. The process by which they are healed is, for Toru, both passive and sexual; as he sits blindfolded in a darkened room, his mind blank, the women kiss, fondle, and caress the mark on his cheek.

But the structure of the third narrative is more complex than this, for it encompasses both the physical and metaphysical aspects of the central narrative (Toru and Kumiko) in its focus on sexuality and the unconscious, and at the same time brings to bear the historical significance of the World War II, the power of the State, and the risks of playing with the inner consciousness.

CINNAMON AND THE LABYRINTH

Most of this third narrative is revealed to us through Nutmeg's mute son, Cinnamon, a refined youth of about twenty. Through certain asides, unattributed, we learn that Cinnamon lost his ability to speak through a strange incident that occurred when he was very young. Waking one night to investigate the cry of a bird he has never heard before, he spots two men, one of whom looks just like his father, burying a small bag under a tree in the family's garden. The man who looks like his father climbs the tree, never to return. After watching for a while he goes back to bed, but later dreams that he has gone out to the garden to dig up the bag, which turns out to contain a human heart, still beating.

When he returns to bed, he finds another "him" sleeping in his bed. He panics, fearing that if there is another "him," then he himself will no longer have a place in the world. In order to preserve his existence, he forces his way into the bed with the other "him" and goes to sleep. When he wakes the next morning, he discovers that he no longer possesses a voice.

From this time on the boy—later known to us as Cinnamon— seems to live in two worlds: one that is shared by his mother and other family members; and another, inner world of his own. Later we come to suspect that this "inner world" is the same as the unconscious hotel in which Toru seeks Kumiko. For Cinnamon this takes the form of cyberspace, the mysterious interior of his computer network, to which he gradually allows Toru (limited) access.

There is no question of what that inner space means to Cinnamon: it is the key, if he can only unlock it, to the meaning of his life, and the answer to why his voice was taken from him. To do this, Cinnamon creates stories (again, the power of the story is revealed!). This is a practice first begun with his mother, who used to play a game with him of making up stories about her own father, a veterinarian with the Imperial Army in Manchuria who bore a mark on his right cheek virtually identical to Toru's. How much truth there is in the stories they create is impossible to say, for Nutmeg's father disappeared after the Soviet invasion in the last days of the war. But this is not the point; these stories, which are

connected with those of Mamiya and Honda in their expression of
tension between individual Japanese soldiers and the Japanese central command, are designed not to reinvent the life of the actual
man who was Cinnamon's grandfather, but to help Cinnamon to
understand (and *create*) himself. Toru recognizes this after having
been permitted a brief glimpse at one of the stories in Cinnamon's
computer.

I had no way of telling how much of the story was true. Was every bit of it
Cinnamon's creation, or were parts of it based on actual events?

I would probably have to read all sixteen stories to find the answers to my
questions, but even after a single reading of #8, I had some idea, however
vague, of what Cinnamon was looking for in his writing. He was engaged
in a serious search for the meaning of his own existence. And he was
hoping to find it by looking into the events that had preceded his own
birth. (528–529)

The stories, no doubt at least nominally grounded in those his
mother had told him about his grandfather, are filled with the
violence and misery of the final weeks in Manchuria, during which
the Imperial Army, hopelessly outnumbered, prepared to make its
last stand against the Soviet armored units assembling for their final
assault on them. The first story concerns the killing of animals at
the Hsin-Ching Zoo in order to prevent them from being acciden-
tally released once the Soviets have invaded. This task is assigned to
an intelligent young lieutenant who has no stomach for the job,
and in the end leaves it only partially completed.

We gain a better sense of the lieutenant's attitude toward the war
and his role in it in a later story in which he is given the job of
executing eight Chinese prisoners, members of the local military
academy's baseball team who have attempted to flee the city in its

final days. The lieutenant's impressions, conveyed to the veterinarian (Nutmeg's father) are similar to those of "Hamano" in Mamiya's earlier narrative.

"Just between you and me, I think the order stinks. What the hell good is it going to do to kill these guys? We don't have any planes left, we don't have any warships, our best troops are dead. Some kind of special new bomb wiped out the whole city of Hiroshima in a split second. . . . We've already killed a lot of Chinese, and adding a few bodies to the count isn't going to make any difference. But orders are orders." (522)

In this brief statement, the lieutenant expresses the "tension between individuals and the state" that interests Murakami so much. What is one to do when given orders that make no sense, that merely reassert the stupid brutality of those in charge? Much of the brutality of the war, he suggests, is attributable not to individuals, but to the State that commands them.

Another important aspect of Cinnamon's subnarrative on the computer is its recreation of the "wind-up bird" itself, linking the narrative to earlier phases of the novel. The wind-up bird in Cinnamon's narrative world is a spectral creature, audible only to certain gifted (or cursed) people, and visible to none. Its eerie cry emerges at moments of great tension, such as when the animals at the zoo are shot, or when the Chinese prisoners are executed. Its cry also coincides, roughly, at least, with tiny, parenthetical prophesies about individual characters in the story. We are told, for instance, the final fate of the soldier under the lieutenant's command who can hear the bird's cry.

Finally, we are given the impressions of Cinnamon's grandfather, and these are significant mainly because they tell us more about Cinnamon himself. Observing the executions of the Chinese prisoners, for instance, the veterinarian imagines himself to be split into two distinct halves, both executioner and executed. "The veterinarian watched in numbed silence, overtaken by the sense that he was beginning to split in two. He became simultaneously the stabber and the stabbed. He could feel both the impact of the bayonet as it entered his victim's body and the pain of having his internal organs slashed to bits" (520). This dualism is equally an aspect of Cinnamon, who was "split in two" at the age of six. It is also a link with others in the novel who have experienced the same thing: Creta Kano, Kumiko, Nutmeg, and indeed Toru himself. At the same time, it provides a physical, visceral quality to that sensation, linking it to the skinning of Yamamoto, and eventually to the murder of Nutmeg's husband, whose body is found with all its internal organs missing.

The third narrative, then, manages to bring together many of the disparate elements of the first two: the clashing historical periods, the dichotomy between physical and metaphysical, the gap between the conscious and unconscious worlds. It even gives a common metaphorical reading, in the form of the computer, to the mystery of the unconscious. Cinnamon's narrative manages to close the gaps between the three narratives, tying together elements that appeared unrelated at the end of the first two books.

By this time it must be reasonably clear that what really connects the three disparate narratives that make up *The Wind-up Bird Chronicle* is a crisis of identity that is both physical and metaphysical, real and magical. It is born of the separation, so to speak, of the various elements that make up one's identity: a "core" identity that resides within one, and the sum of one's experiences and interactions with others. Identity is, naturally, tied to the individual will, but in this novel that will is constantly threatened by the controlling power of the State and its organs. In that sense the work can be read as a quasi-political novel, one of resistance to the State. On a more basic level, however, the novel depicts a more archetypal conflict between good and evil, the resolution of which has the potential to return fertility to the wasteland.

IDENTITY AND THE UNCONSCIOUS IN MURAKAMI

It should be borne in mind that identity in Murakami fiction is as much a physical thing as it is an abstract concept of the mind. That is to say, while identity is constructed of one's memories, experiences and personality traits, it also has a *physical* manifestation in the author's world, endowed with a real, tangible quality. Its existence is asserted again and again in Murakami's work, and the way he characterizes it is consistent enough that it merits some discussion here.

Identity for Murakami is always a combination of two primary elements: the conscious self—the person we know as ourselves in daily life; and the unconscious "other," a mysterious alter ego who dwells in the depths of our unconscious. These two sides of our identity ideally share the task of identity formation, but perform different roles. The conscious self, as might be expected, encounters new situations and acts upon them, providing experiences to be processed by the unconscious "other;" the inner self, or "other," then processes these experiences into memories, simultaneously creating links between the various other memories that are stored in the unconscious. In simple terms, the conscious self tells the unconscious other what it sees, and the unconscious "other" tells the conscious "self" what that means in light of previous experiences.

The relationship between these "sides" is a symbiotic one; both are necessary for the construction of a solid identity. The two are virtual opposites, yet neither can stand alone. Together, they form— and then control—what might be called the "core identity," or "core consciousness," of the individual. This "core" is the source of identity, the heart and soul of the individual. May Kasahara describes it as a kind of "heat source" that keeps us living: " 'Everybody's born with some different thing at the core of their existence," she tells Toru. "And that thing, whatever it is, becomes like a heat source that runs each person from the inside' " (324).

This is the most important aspect of identity in Murakami, and lies at the heart of every movement and desire of the Murakami hero. That is to say, the recurring motif in Murakami fiction is the hero's desire to come into contact with that "something" that lies at the core of his identity, to know more about it. At the same time, to come into contact with this "core" engenders a certain risk, for in so doing one threatens to influence, even alter, the essential nature of the thing, leaving one in doubt as to who one really is.

Fortunately for Murakami characters, that "core identity" is well protected, guarded by heavy walls within the mind. It is sometimes described by the author as a "black box," something like the flight data recorder on modern aircraft. Armored against tampering, fire, and the force of impact in a crash, the black box is designed to retain its information regardless of what is done to it. Only when it is opened does it become corrupted.

Of course, it can always be removed from the aircraft. Once this is done, the machine from which it has been removed will no longer carry any record of where it has been, or what it has done.

This may seem like an odd metaphor for human identity, but it is an appropriate one for the identity crises suffered by the characters described in the three narratives above. It is what happens to Creta Kano, for instance, whose "defilement" by Noboru Wataya is both physical and psychological. Reaching directly into Creta Kano's body, Noboru splits her in two, then draws out the "core" of her identity, leaving her empty and lost. We cannot fail to note here the very physical manifestation of that "core."

"Out from between the two cleanly split halves of my physical self came crawling a thing that I had never seen or touched before. How large it was I could not tell, but it was as wet and slippery as a newborn baby. I had absolutely no idea what it was. It had always been inside me, and yet it was something of which I had no knowledge. This man had drawn it out of me." (303)

Like other characters who suffer this fate, Creta Kano wants desperately to see for herself what this "something" is — to know it firsthand, and thus *know who she really is*. But no one is ever permitted to know this. Malta Kano says much the same thing, a little cryptically: we are never permitted to see ourselves directly; we must rely on the gaze of another (an "other") to tell us what it looks like. " 'One cannot look directly at one's own face with one's own eyes, for example. One has no choice but to look at one's reflection in the mirror. Through experience, we come to *believe* that the image is correct, but that is all' " (284).

Creta Kano's experience, at once a physical and a metaphysical one, helps us to understand a little better some of the other physical mutilations in the story. We might comprehend, for instance, the murder of Nutmeg's husband, whose body is found with all its internal organs removed and the face slashed to bits, as a similar, brutally physical attempt to remove both his external identity (his face) and his internal "core" (his organs). Murakami's focus on the organs in the abdominal cavity *does* have some cultural significance here that is worth noting. Unlike in the West, where the soul is thought to exist in the mind, or sometimes in the heart, Japanese tradition has it that the center of one's being exists in the belly. This, according to some, is the origin of *seppuku*, "belly cutting," known in the West as "hara-kiri." Opening the abdomen by disembowelment literally opens the true essence of the individual, and thus is taken as a last demonstration of truth. This may help us to understand the executions of the Chinese baseball players in Cinnamon's story; looking beyond the practical reasons for bayonetting the prisoners (to save ammunition), the mutilation of their internal organs tears to pieces their "core selves" as well as their bodies. It may also help explain why, despite having been beaten to death with a baseball bat, the last victim of this massacre still manages to sit up and grab the veterinarian by the hand (524). His "core" has not yet been fully extinguished, and that "something" within him still struggles to exert its own existence.

We gain a very clear picture of the physical side of the core identity quite early in the story from May Kasahara as well. She describes it as the "lump of death," but in the context of the above discussion we can understand that she really refers to the "core identity" itself.

"... the lump of death. I'm sure there must be something like that. Something round and squishy, like a softball, with a hard little core of dead nerves. . . . It's squishy on the outside, and the deeper you go inside, the harder it gets . . . and the closer you get to the center, the harder the squishy stuff gets, until you reach this tiny core. It's sooo tiny, like a tiny ball bearing, and really hard." (20–21)

It is this "something" (*nani ka*, an expression that recurs throughout the novel) that obsesses everyone in the story. Mamiya, despite his obviously unpleasant associations with wells, still feels the urge to climb down into any well he sees. Why? "I probably continue to hope that I will encounter *something* down there," he tells Toru, "that if I go down inside and simply wait, it will be possible for me to encounter a certain *something*. . . . What I hope to find is the meaning of the life that I have lost. By what was it taken away from me, and why?" (349; my emphasis). These are almost the same words used by Creta Kano in describing her experience with Noboru Wataya.

In sum, then, *The Wind-up Bird Chronicle* is about the "core" identity of the individual, how it can be located, understood, protected, or alternately, removed or destroyed. It also lies at the heart of Kumiko's disappearance for, as we later discover, Kumiko's inner core has also been tampered with, leaving her lost, uncertain of who, or where, she really is.

DIVIDING THE SELF, APPROACHING THE CORE

We now approach one of the really difficult aspects of this novel: the question of how the core identity is corrupted. The process is, I believe, one of division. That is, the entire Self (conscious "self" and unconscious "other") is divided in two, and from between them, the "core" is removed. Without this essential link to the central body of memory and information there can be no real connection between them, and thus no possibility of the necessary communication that creates a "whole" person.

This is what has happened to Kumiko. Like Creta Kano, she has been stripped of her core identity, leaving her conscious and unconscious selves divided and lost. One exists somewhere in the conscious realm — we never learn where — while the other lives in the unconscious, the mysterious hotel, in "Room 208."

We cannot help noticing the opposite nature of these two sides of the same person. The Kumiko known to Toru as his wife, for instance, seems to be a perfectly ordinary young woman, an intelligent professional, leading a reasonably normal married life with him. But her unconscious "other" is a mirror image of this Kumiko, sexually charged and driven by pure physical desire. This "other" that has always lurked within Kumiko has remained suppressed by the conscious Kumiko, but is nevertheless a critical part of her. What Noboru has done in removing her core identity is to eliminate the central reference point by which the conscious Kumiko keeps this unconscious side of herself under control. Thus released, the "other" Kumiko is free to express herself in a characteristically sexual way. In one sense this is healthy; Toru's wife confesses that she never found sexual fulfillment with him, perhaps because she maintained such a tight control over her "darker side." At the same time, however, it leaves her conscious self in a weakened position of submission, helpless against the power of her inner sexual desire.

Toru, of course, takes on the role of saving Kumiko from this fate, but his task is complicated by the fact that he too must struggle against the power of his unconscious "other." Compounding the difficulty of this task is the fact that this "other side" of Toru is Noboru himself.

THE "NOSTALGIC IMAGE"

This leads to an interesting question: If the "other" exists in the realm of the unconscious, how then does Toru encounter his own "other" in the conscious world? The answer lies in the concept of the "nostalgic image," something I have discussed at length in several previous writings on Murakami.

The concept of the nostalgic image is fairly straightforward, but demands a leap of faith on the part of readers, because it is heavily dependent on the magical elements in the text. It refers to a recurring motif in Murakami fiction in which the protagonist longs desperately for someone or something he has lost — a friend, a lover, an object — and in response, his unconscious mind, using his memories of the object or person in question, creates a likeness, or a surrogate, which then appears in the conscious world as a character in the story. There is, however, one major catch: nothing ever really looks quite the same in both worlds. Thus, to the protagonist as well as the hapless reader of Murakami fiction, the relationship between the "nostalgic image" character and its origin is often obscure. This much is hinted in the final lines of *Hear the Wind Sing*, in a quote ostensibly from Friedrich Nietzsche: "We can never comprehend the depths of the gloom of night in the light of day" (*Murakami Haruki Zensakuhin 1979–1989*, 1:120). In the context of Murakami's fictional world this means that nothing passes from the unconscious into the conscious world without experiencing some kind of radical transformation in appearance.

Nevertheless, we can usually spot these "image characters" by their peculiarity: nameless twins and a talking pinball machine in Murakami's second novel, *Pinball, 1973* (1980); the "Sheepman," made up of the protagonist's unconscious conceptions of Rat and the Sheep in *A Wild Sheep Chase*; the strange little people, some seven-tenths of normal size, who invade the home of a man in the short story "TV People;" the opaque image of a middle-aged woman who appears on the protagonist's back in "The Story of the Poor Aunt;" and so on.

Forming the connection between the unconscious memory and the image it becomes is usually a matter of linguistic relationship. For instance, a dead girlfriend from the protagonist's student days named Naoko reappears as a pinball machine known as "the Spaceship." The connection lies in the fact that Naoko used to tell him stories about people on other planets. In the same novel, the protagonist's missing friend "Rat" emerges as "the Twins," nameless girls who suddenly turn up on either side of him one morning after a night of heavy drinking. In attempting to find some suitable names for them (reminding us of Nutmeg and Cinnamon!), the protagonist comes up with "Entrance" and "Exit," which leads him to think about things without exits, such as mousetraps, and this finally leads to Rat.

Similar "image characters" appear in *The Wind-up Bird Chronicle*. It is possible to read the characters of Creta and Malta Kano, for instance, as images of Kumiko and her older sister, a character Toru knows only through Kumiko's stories of her. The relationships and experiences are similar. Kumiko, for instance, suggests that she might have handled her difficult childhood better had her sister not died, thus denying her a confidant; Creta Kano, on the other hand, describes her own trials with pain, attempted suicide, and identity crisis in the absence of *her* sister, who was performing mystical divinations on the island of Malta during these critical years. We note also the various incarnations of Creta Kano—one living in pain, another in numbness, and finally one who balances the two—and perhaps think of the two "sides" of Kumiko: one who is "numb" to Toru's sexual caresses, and another caught up in a torrent of uncontrollable sexual abandon.

Other clues, a little more prosaic, also suggest a correlation between Kumiko and Creta. The fact that Creta Kano is exactly the same size as Kumiko and is thus able to slip into her clothing with no difficulty is suggestive. We might also note the retro-look affected by Creta Kano that suggests her roots in a previous time; she is a mixture of Kumiko past and present. Finally, there is the slippage in identity between Creta and the "Telephone Woman"/Kumiko during their sexual encounter with Toru in the unconscious hotel room.

But more than anything it is the similarity of her experience with Kumiko's—and the central role of Noboru Wataya—that is suspicious. The scene in which Noboru draws out Creta Kano's core consciousness, for instance, has the unmistakable signs of childbirth, or of an abortive birth. Might the "defilement" of Creta not actually be another way of looking at the operation in which Kumiko's own fertility is negated? Finally, there is the dream in which

Malta Kano tells Toru that her sister has given birth to a baby, and named it Corsica; this, Toru tells May Kasahara at the end of the novel, is what he will call his own baby if he and Kumiko should have one.

Another character who bears a strong image quality is "Ushikawa," an unsavory little man who acts as go-between for Toru and Noboru in the latter stages of the book. Readers of *A Wild Sheep Chase* will certainly recognize similarities between this man, whom Toru describes as "without question, one of the ugliest human beings I had ever encountered . . . less like an actual human being than like something from a long-forgotten nightmare" (431), and the "Sheepman," whose unkempt appearance is the more unique for the fact that he walks around in an ill-fitting, poorly-stitched sheep suit.

But the point is less their grotesque appearance than their function. Just as the "Sheepman" is a combination of Rat and the antagonist Sheep, "Ushikawa" seems to be created out of Kumiko, on the one hand, and his arch-nemesis Noboru, on the other. The association with Kumiko helps us to understand both "Ushikawa's" evident closeness to her (" 'I'm taking care of her,' " he tells Toru cryptically on p. 433), and yet his lack of knowledge about the details of her imprisonment ("Not even I know the all the details," ibid.). The connection to Noboru (who, lest we forget, is also part of Toru) accounts for his violent side, expressed in how he used to beat his wife and children (435). We can also hear the warning, megalomaniacal tones of Noboru in "Ushikawa's" assertion that Noboru "has a very real kind of power that he can exercise in this world, a power that grows stronger every day" (437). This is Noboru speaking directly to Toru.

THE "OTHER" STRIKES BACK: WHO IS NOBORU WATAYA?

If Noboru Wataya really is Toru's "other" self, as I have suggested, however, then his antagonistic nature makes him something of an anomaly. Whereas in other Murakami fiction the unconscious "other" has always been a benign existence whose aim is to help the conscious protagonist discover himself, in this novel the "other" is fiercely hostile to Toru. The reason for this is not difficult to discern, however: whereas "self" and "other" maintain a healthy, symbiotic relationship when living in their respective worlds, here the "other" has broken out of the unconscious realm, and seeks to coexist with Toru in "this" world. Since by its nature the two aspects of the Self cannot live together in the same place, Noboru's emergence into Toru's conscious world can only bring trouble. No one makes this clearer than Creta Kano:

"Noboru Wataya is a person who belongs to a world that is the exact opposite of yours," said Creta Kano. Then she seemed to be searching for the words she needed to continue. "In a world where you are losing everything, Mr. Okada, Noboru Wataya is gaining everything. In a world where you are rejected, he is accepted. And the opposite is just as true. Which is why he hates you so intensely." (314)

Toru seems to understand this much himself, particularly in his inability simply to ignore Noboru's existence. "I can distinguish between myself and another as beings of two different realms," he notes early in the book. "When someone gets on my nerves, the first thing I do is transfer the object of my unpleasant feelings to another domain, one having no connection with me" (78). But with Noboru this is not possible. "I was simply unable to shove Noboru Wataya into a domain having no connection with me" (79). Why should this be, if not for the fact that Noboru is a part of him, and he can never entirely ignore or run away from himself?

As Creta Kano says, Noboru is the opposite of himself, existing in a "different world." This opposition is manifested in their behavior throughout the novel; whereas Toru is a mild, passive, unobtrusive figure, Noboru is violent, dominant, and ambitious. Yet there is crossover, or rather, there are points when this dark, violent side overcomes him, just as Kumiko's dark, sexual side gradually takes hold of her. We see Toru lose control of himself in the scene when he beats the guitar player with his own baseball bat.

My mind was telling me to stop: This was enough. Any more would be too much. The man could no longer get to his feet. But I couldn't stop. There were two of me now, I realized. I had split in two, but *this* me had lost the power to stop the other me. (338)

This enraged Toru is, one supposes, a manifestation of Noboru, who gains strength in the darkness and takes control of Toru's actions in the real world. We might note in passing that Toru's description above is almost identical to "Ushikawa's" monologue about beating his wife and children, hinting at the connection between them:

"I'd try to stop myself, but I couldn't. I couldn't control myself. After a certain point I would tell myself that I had done enough damage, that I had to stop, but I didn't know how to stop." (435)

The object of "Ushikawa's" beating vis-a-vis the object of Toru's is not important here; what matters is the expression of uncontrollable violence, for as Toru listens to "Ushikawa," he really confronts himself.

IMAGE AND ARTIFICE

If Noboru Wataya is indeed an "image" character, then his emergence as a politician and television commentator are particularly appropriate for this role. Interestingly, his artificiality is obvious to Toru even when meeting Noboru face-to-face:

[L]ooking at his face was like looking at a television image. He talked the way people on television talked, and he moved the way people on television moved. There was always a layer of glass between us. I was on this side, and he was on that side. (199)

Noboru's ideas, according to Toru, are equally phony, though they take in the vast majority of the people. "[I]f you paid close attention to what he was saying or what he had written, you knew that his words lacked consistency. They reflected no single worldview based on profound conviction" (75). For Toru, who detests artifice so profoundly that he feels uncomfortable even putting on a suit for his meeting with Malta Kano, such chicanery is intolerable, and for this reason as much as any other his attitude toward Noboru has a touch of extremism in it: as he tells Ushikawa, " 'I don't simply dislike him: I cannot accept the fact of his very existence' " (438).

VIOLENCE AND SEXUALITY

The oppositional relationship between Noboru Wataya and Toru Okada is, as I suggested earlier, observable most of all in their respective approaches to sexuality. If indeed the two men represent diametric oppositions — dominance vs. passivity, ambition vs. modesty, artifice vs. sincerity — then this is demonstrated in their practice of sexuality as well, a fact that is particularly critical in *The Wind-up Bird Chronicle*, in which sexuality is the means both to destroying, and also to restoring, the "core consciousness." The negative effects of sexual violence are visible in Noboru's attempt to take control of Creta Kano, resulting in the loss of her identity, and something similar presumably happened to Kumiko's elder sister, causing her to commit suicide. A rampant, dominating sexuality is also at the root of Kumiko's disappearance, as we have seen. At the center of each of these incidents stands Noboru Wataya, whose sexual energy expresses itself in destructive ways.

An entirely different aspect of sexuality is seen, however, in the work that Toru performs at the "clinic" operated by Nutmeg and Cinnamon Akasaka. As the healer of internally unbalanced women, Toru's role is to help a very élite clientele to restore something that is missing from their inner selves. And yet, though I call this "work," his role is wholly a passive one, that of a medium through which the women establish contact with the "shared consciousness" in which so much of this novel is played out. Toru's ability to serve as medium is grounded in the mark on his cheek, literally a sign on his face that he has access to that place, and carries a tiny conduit to it. His work is also aided by his growing skill at dividing his mind from his body, much as Creta Kano does. Through him, as a result, psychic energy flows between the two worlds, a mysterious source of healing for those in whom that flow has been disrupted. One might say that by establishing direct contact with that flow of psychic energy, his patients are able to restart the flow within themselves.

The process *sounds* simple enough: Toru sits in a darkened room, his eyes covered with dark goggles, and he allows his mind to empty until he has entered a state of existence between the conscious and unconscious worlds. While he sits in this state of repose, the clients touch and manipulate the mark on his cheek, establishing direct contact with the "other world" of the shared unconscious. What they find there is impossible to say with certainty, but we sense that they touch, fleetingly, that mysterious "heat source" that lies at the center of their existence as individuals, and find temporary peace.

But the operation is also unquestionably sexual. While Toru sits utterly still and passive, the women essentially make love to the mark on his cheek, causing him to climax.

She then stood up, came around behind me, and instead of her fingertips, used her tongue . . . she licked my mark. . . . With varying pressure, changing angles, and different movement, [her tongue] tasted and sucked and stimulated my mark. I felt a hot, moist throbbing below the waist. I didn't want to have an erection. To do so would have been all too meaningless. But I couldn't stop myself. (372)

But this is by no means a "meaningless" joining, for in his passive role as sexual stimulus/unconscious conduit, Toru mirrors in reverse the violent, penetrating assaults of Noboru, whose violent sexuality has the effect of destroying the flow between the conscious and unconscious, closing off the necessary movement between inner and outer selves, and thus, in figurative terms, shattering the fertile relationship between the two worlds in which identity and individual selfhood develop.

This helps us to understand better the nature of Toru's sexual relations with Creta Kano, as well. We note, for example, that in both of their sexual encounters Toru takes the less aggressive role: Creta fellates him in the first instance, while in the second he lies on his back as *she* mounts *him*, foreshadowing his task as healer. The result is that the two of them share some metaphysical aspect of their inner selves with one another. They literally bring their inner "cores" into contact with one another, establishing a flow of energy that allows them to communicate in a mystical way. "It felt as if something inside her, something special inside her, were slowing working its way through my organ into me," says Toru. At the same time, something of Toru's — a part of his "core," perhaps — works *its* way into Creta Kano, helping her to rid herself of the sense of defilement left behind by Noboru.

The same thing, on a slightly more chaste level, occurs between Toru and May Kasahara: a "flow" is established between them that allows their core identities, however fleetingly, to come into contact with each other. As Toru rests in the sunshine with her shortly after the appearance of the mark on his cheek, his eyes closed, May Kasahara begins to kiss the mark on his cheek, just as Nutmeg's customers will later do. At the same time, she places his hand on a nearly-healed cut over her eye, received in her recent motorcycle accident. While she applies her tongue to his mark, Toru strokes the wound on her face, and as he does so, "the waves of her consciousness pulsed through my fingertips and into me — a delicate resonance of longing" (327–328).

Surely this is the point of the entire book, the one act that can save the world, this contact between the core identities on the individual level. May Kasahara certainly senses it. Her greatest desire, aside from understanding more about the core that lurks within her, is to share her awareness of its existence with someone else. " 'What I'd really like to do is find a way to communicate that feeling to another person,' " she tells Toru immediately before the scene described above. " 'But I can't seem to do it. They just don't get it. Of course, the problem could be that I'm not explaining it very well . . . ' " (324).

The real problem, of course, is that she tries to convey in words what can only be experienced through the senses. How can one explain what can only be felt through the pulsing flow of pure energy?

WATER AND FLOW

The word "flow" occurs more than once in the above section, and not by accident, for with the possible exception of sexuality, there is no more important motif in this novel than flow and water.

As a symbol, of course, water has a number of meanings that might be considered orthodox in literary circles: it can represent the flow of time, not unlike sand in an hourglass; it can represent fertility, the origin of all life; it can suggest constant change (one can never look twice at the "same" river); it can indicate cyclicity, in the sense that water flows to the sea, is drawn up into the clouds, and falls again to the earth, eventually returning to the river to make its way to the sea again; and so forth.

The Wind-up Bird Chronicle makes use of all of these conventional readings of water, and while Murakami likes to claim not to know what his own symbolism means (the "wind-up bird" is a case in point!), water is one symbol that he understands well, and carefully crafts from one end of the novel to the other. Indeed, without too much difficulty we can read this entire novel as a "river of narrative," occasionally obstructed (at which point the narrative stops, as at the end of Book Two), sometimes flowing rapidly and violently. The river of narrative, like a real river, flows sometimes above the ground, and sometimes beneath it. Perhaps most importantly, especially as a metaphor for time, most rivers meander in places, giving the impression of flowing in more than one direction. This may help us to envision, shortly below, how time operates in the story.

We are clear on the critical importance of water and flow from the earliest stages in the text. Malta Kano, for instance, tells Toru that " 'something has obstructed the flow' " around his house (43), though whether she refers to real water or simply some metaphor of it is difficult to say. Later in the book, Toru recalls the cautionary advice of Honda, who warns him to beware of water. Sounding like a Buddhist sermon, Honda prophesies the conflict between Toru and Noboru, the roots of which lie in resisting the natural flow of things. " 'If you resist the flow, everything dries up. If everything dries up, the world is darkness' " (51).

Taken in the context of the discussion above, we may understand that Noboru obstructs the "flow" that must exist between the conscious and unconscious selves. He closes off the conduits that permit this flow — necessarily a *bidirectional* flow, allowing *interaction* between the two worlds — and thereby inhibits access of the conscious "self" to information held within, while cutting the supply of stimuli needed by the unconscious other to produce memory and experience. The result — darkness, according to Honda — foreshadows Toru's final struggle against Noboru to restore the flow in the pitch dark wasteland of an increasingly dried up unconscious.

The concept of the "wasteland" is an appropriate one here, as once again Murakami relies on a very conventional theme: restoration of fertility to the land. Just as the Arthurian legends tell of the break in faith between the King and the Land that leads to the latter's inability to support the people, so too does Toru struggle to find his own key — his Grail — that will somehow clear the obstruction of the flow and allow the land to breathe again. But the key is not merely to rescue Kumiko, though this is the object of his own quest; rather, it is the destruction of the evil presence of Noboru, a physical embodiment of the blight that poisons the world.

THE WELL: CONDUIT BETWEEN WORLDS

Wells (and other similarly-shaped structures) are a major motif in Murakami fiction as a conduit between the conscious and unconscious worlds. In *Hard-Boiled Wonderland and the End of the World*, for instance, the protagonist's only potential escape route from his unconscious mind is through a pond that appears to flow beneath the walls that enclose the area, presumably bringing him back to the conscious world. In *Dance Dance Dance* (1988) the protagonist boards an elevator in a modern high-rise hotel, but when the doors open finds himself in a much older structure from his past. More recently, the heroine of *The Sputnik Sweetheart*, Sumire, dreams that her long-lost mother comes back from the dead to tell her something, but is sucked into a kind of hollow tower before she can convey her message, leaving Sumire wondering whether to follow her into that world.

The well in *The Wind-up Bird Chronicle* becomes a central point of contention as well, and both Toru and Noboru seem to recognize the importance of controlling this important link between their two worlds. Toru's work as a healer grows directly from his need to own and control the land on which the well is located. Achieving this at least temporarily when Nutmeg purchases the land and holds it in trust for Toru, the well also serves as bait to draw Noboru out, forcing him to bargain. Eventually Noboru even concedes the possibility of returning Kumiko to Toru in exchange for giving up the well, making clear how critical control of this portal between worlds is to him.

Fortunately for Toru (and for us, his loyal cheering section), he maintains possession of the well long enough to accomplish his task, and as he moves from Room 208 to the well for the last time, the well fills with water. Even Toru, by this time, understands the importance of the water that fills the well: "It had been dried up, dead, for such a long time, yet now it had come back to life. Could this have some connection with what I had accomplished *there*? Yes, it probably did. Something might have loosened whatever it was that had been obstructing the vein of water" (592). The fact that he might drown in the well as it fills with water does not seem to trouble him much; "I had brought this well back to life, and I would die in its rebirth. It was not a bad way to die, I told myself" (593).

But Toru, as we know, is rescued in the end by Cinnamon, and this leaves us with one interesting question: How will Toru maintain his *own* identity if his unconscious "other" no longer exists? Are we to imagine that the Noboru Wataya in his unconscious mind is still alive somewhere, back where he belongs? On this one point we might, perhaps, quibble with Murakami's decision to save his hero from death at the end of the novel.

In terms of the overall quest of *The Wind-up Bird Chronicle*, then, the novel provides a successful conclusion. By beating his "other" to death in the unconscious world Toru has achieved his goal, and if proof is required, Murakami provides it in the restoration of the well—Toru's own private conduit to the "other world"—with the real flow of water—significantly, *warm* water, offering the promise of new life.

WHAT IS THAT CONFOUNDED WIND-UP BIRD?

I noted above that the "flow" that is so important as a metaphor for life and fertility is also a metaphor for time, and this brings us, at last, to the "wind-up bird" itself. The wind-up bird is, of course, an "open" symbol, like Melville's whale, and can thus be read simultaneously in a number of ways.

Toru himself offers several suggestions within the narrative. Upon reading Cinnamon's "Wind-up Bird Chronicle #8," for instance, he suggests that the bird is a harbinger of doom, a source of deadly fate. "The cry of this bird was audible only to certain special people, who were guided by it toward inescapable ruin" (529). In this sense, the bird takes on a god-like role, as controller of human destiny. People, according to this suggestion, are like puppets set in motion for the bird's amusement, or, as Toru puts it, like wind-up dolls.

People were no more than dolls set on tabletops, the springs in their backs wound up tight, dolls set to move in ways they could not choose, moving in directions they could not choose. Nearly all within range of the wind-up bird's cry were ruined, lost. Most of them died, plunging over the edge of the table. (530)

Based on this reading we might see the wind-up bird as symbolic of the power of the State itself, manipulating and using the people in ways they cannot control. Indeed, this is the essential structure of *A Wild Sheep Chase*, in which the Sheep, a source of unimaginable power, takes control of the weak-minded and rules human destiny through them. It is thought, in that book, to have been the source of the military genius of Ghenghis Khan, as well as the root of power in elements of the Japanese State during the World War II.

If we choose to view the wind-up bird in this sense, then Noboru's "special power" to take control of people's core identities is surely connected to it. As a politician, a representative of political power in Japan, Noboru's transformation from a sloppy, socially inept college professor into a slick, yet artificial, politician could easily be attributed to some mysterious relationship with the wind-up bird.

This is a plausible reading of the wind-up bird, and could be pursued in much greater depth than is possible in this volume. But I wish to offer an alternative reading, one that takes into account the motif of flow and time. I wish to read the "wind-up bird" as a metaphor for time and history.

Toru himself offers a reading of the bird in this way from the earliest part of the novel: the bird's real function, he believes, is to "wind the spring of our quiet little world" (9). In other words, the turning of the world—and its attendant creation of "time"—rests in the hands of this mystical bird, whose task is to keep time flowing forward, creating temporal distance between past and present.

But the springs, like all springs, do wind down, and must be rewound by the bird. These are the points at which the bird's cry is heard, and also the moments of tension in the novel, when disparate worlds seem to crash into one another. The bird's cry is heard when historical moments—past and present, present and future—slam into one another as a result of the loss of momentum in time. According to this reading, the bird is not the *cause* of catastrophe, then, but naturally appears in order to set the flow of time going again. This may help us to understand the prophesies that appear at various points in the book: Cinnamon's discovery of the buried heart, prophesying the death and mutilation of his father; the various parenthetical prophesies concerning the soldiers in Manchuria; and even Honda's prophetic warnings to Toru and Mamiya.

This also allows us to comprehend better why May Kasahara nicknames Toru "Mr. Wind-up Bird"; his function, like the bird's, is to restore the "flow," reestablishing a fertile relationship between "self" and "other." In this context, he and the "wind-up bird" may have more in common than he realizes.

CONCLUSIONS

Like the well, filling at last with water at the end of the novel, the human "self" is characterized as a vessel into which stimuli are poured like water, to be stirred in the crucible of the unconscious, processed into the memories and experiences that make us who we are. When this process is permitted to continue smoothly, according to the flow of energy back and forth between the two modes of consciousness, human identity is stable and secure.

But, as we have seen, identity does not always work so smoothly. Human identity in this novel is altogether too fragile, too vulnerable to removal, transport, or even destruction. It can be replaced by another. When Cinnamon awakens from his terrifying dream of seeing another "him" sleeping in his bed, for instance, he intuitively understands that his "self" has been placed into another body that looks like his own, but is not. "He felt as if his self had been put into a new container. . . . There was something about this one, he felt, that just didn't match his original self" (425).

At the same time, identity that has been lost can also be recreated. Creta Kano has suffered a catastrophe even greater than Cinnamon's, and now describes herself as "empty," but she is rebuilding her identity, piece by piece. " 'I am quite literally empty. I am just getting started, putting some contents into this empty container little by little" (313), she tells Toru, for " 'Without a true self . . . a person can not go on living. It is like the ground we stand on' " (308). Like the well that fills with water at the end, all of the victims of *The Wind-up Bird Chronicle* attempt to refill the empty vessels left behind after their core identities have been removed. Some, like Creta Kano and Cinnamon, are partially successful; others, such as Mamiya, end in dismal failure.

Whether the central quest to "save" Kumiko will be successful is left uncertain as of novel's end. Toru has reestablished contact with her by the end of the work, but we cannot say whether she will ever be able to reconstruct her identity. An educated guess might lead us to believe (or at least to hope) that Toru *will* recover Kumiko and, following the restoration of fertility he has achieved, that they will have a child together. " 'If Kumiko and I have a child, I'm thinking of naming it Corsica' " (609), he tells May Kasahara, again returning to what Malta tells him in his dream. If my reading above is correct, and if Creta Kano and Kumiko are indeed one and the same, then Malta Kano's words are the final prophesy in this book, and a harbinger of healing and restoration.

3

The Novel's Reception

GENERAL REVIEW COVERAGE

Reviews of *The Wind-up Bird Chronicle* were mixed, but more positive than not. Most reviewers found something to admire in the work, though some expressed disappointment in the lack of closure at the end. A very few felt the work was dull. *The Wind-up Bird Chronicle*, in short, was a success, but not an unmitigated one. In this section I would like to look at a few particularly good reviews (and one or two that did not quite make the cut), to present some of the representative views of the novel.

THE LACK OF CLOSURE

One of the more astute readings of the work comes from Michiko Kakutani in the *New York Times Book Review* (Oct. 31, 1997). Kakutani's feelings are clearly mixed about the novel, but her readings are in general on the mark. Calling the novel "wildly ambitious," the chief flaw Kakutani finds is the work's lack of cohesiveness as a narrative work of art. She notes, for instance, that while the work is structured (vaguely, at least) along the lines of the detective novel, it nevertheless fails to achieve the kind of clarity in its ending—a solid, comprehensible solution to the mystery—that such novels normally provide. "No doubt," writes Kakutani, "he means to subvert the conventional detective story and, in doing so, suggest that the world is a mysterious place, that the lines between reality and fantasy are porous, that reason and logic are useless tools in an incomprehensible world."

This is an insightful reading, and Kakutani (perhaps unwittingly) has put her finger on one of central motivations in all Murakami fiction. It is a structural motif that we may see in much of the author's previous fiction as well. Commenting in 1994 on whether *A Wild Sheep Chase* and *Hard-Boiled Wonderland and the End of the World* were intentionally subverted detective stories, Murakami had the following to say:

What I don't like about detective fiction is when the detective solves the mystery. That's always the most boring part. It's boring. So I wanted to leave that out of [*A Wild Sheep Chase*]. What I really wanted to write was a mystery *without* a solution. (Interview with Murakami)

Murakami *does* want to create a mystery that has a greater depth of *reality* to it, and thus he defends the ending of *The Wind-up Bird Chronicle* in the same way:

Have you ever read the Ellery Queen mysteries? There is always a point where he talks to the reader. At that point the writer and the reader are on the same ground. But after that point the thing is solved. And that's *boring*! It isn't real. Mysteries are real. But the solution is not real. (Interview with Murakami)

Generally speaking, Kakutani's critique is justified, and has been echoed by other critics as well. At the same time, her disappointment at the lack of closure may be grounded in assumptions and expectations that can never really be fulfilled in Murakami fiction. She wishes to read *The Wind-up Bird Chronicle* as art, and in this she is bound to be frustrated. "[F]or most of us," writes Kakutani, "art is supposed to do something more than simply mirror the confusions of the world." But herein she misses two fundamental points: first, that Murakami intentionally rejects the notion that his fiction is to be read as art; and second, that the kind of closure she seeks in the "conventional detective story" is precisely what sets that form *apart* from art. If, as has been argued in a number of critical studies on the subject, "art" tends more toward the mimetic portrayal of the world — including its messy incomprehensibility — then the conventional detective story presents the world more as we *wish* it could be, with clear-cut solutions to all the questions raised in the story.

Having said that, however, we should recall Murakami's own contention that his writing is not art, nor has he ever intended for it to be read as such. In a comment given wider exposure to the English-speaking world by its inclusion in one of Jay Rubin's early essays on Murakami, the protagonist of *Hear the Wind Sing* says, "If you seek art and literature, read the Greeks" (*Murakami Haruki Zensakuhin 1979–1989*, 1:11; Cf. Rubin 1990, 387). Literary art, the author claims, whether it exists in the present or not, has no relevance to the everyday world of his readers.

What he *does* believe in, as I said earlier, is the power of the story, of words. For Murakami, the critical aspect of the detective story (or any other fictional formula) is not its sense of closure, but its style. "I've learned a lot from reading the so-called 'genre novels.' The most important thing, to me, is style. . . . You have to grab the reader in the first three or four pages, and to do that you have to have your own strong style" (Interview with Murakami). Read in this context, *The Wind-up Bird Chronicle* may be called "detective fiction" only insofar as it projects this focus on style that is so important to Murakami; its lack of closure, on the other hand, is not a matter of "laziness," as Kakutani has it, but an expression of the author's determination to reflect the real world in his fiction. Still, one is sympathetic to Kakutani's frustration; the lack of conventionality in Murakami's writing is disconcerting, even confusing, to readers unfamiliar with these aspects of his style.

"A WALK AROUND THE BRAIN"

Another review, somewhat less concerned with the chaotic nature of the story, comes from David Mathew, whose more upbeat commentary "On *The Wind-up Bird Chronicle*: Fiction from a Rising Son" came out on-line some months after the novel was released in the United Kingdom in 1999.

Calling *The Wind-up Bird Chronicle* "an incredible achievement," Mathew hits very accurately on the central motivation in the story: "This is a novel which endeavours to explain what it is to be a young man with a flexible approach to his own life: will life break him or merely bend him? What happens when routine is abolished? What does it mean: to be alone?"

Mathew, too, notices the flaws in the novel, and these are unavoidable. The text is, as he notes, "frequently meandering, occasionally baffling, repetitive or overwritten. . . ." This, too, is a regular aspect of Murakami's writing, and it *can* be exasperating. But Mathew also reflects on the fact that Murakami's style is the result of the author's distaste for planning his stories; instead, he allows them to flow directly from his imagination onto the page. "[T]he author is well known to prefer freefalling through his novels, rather than planning, and a certain cumulative force is felt during the reading, possibly as a result of this technique (or lack of technique)," writes Mathew. On this subject, Murakami himself frequently tells interviewers that he himself does not know where his stories will go. Speaking to *Salon* in 1997, the author says of *The Wind-up Bird Chronicle*, "I was enjoying myself writing, because I don't know what going to happen when I take a ride around that corner . . . it's very exciting when you don't know what's going to happen next. The same thing happens to me when I'm writing. It's fun" (Miller, *Salon*, Nov. 24, 1997).

Ultimately, Mathew finds something fresh and exciting in the fact that "*The Wind-up Bird Chronicle* is, by and large, a walk around the lead character's brain," despite the fact that "some of it is disorganized, some of it is unwanted ephemera." But after all, the inner mind is not a well-organized machine, but a place of dark, disturbing forces, containing the roots of identity, but also the potential for madness. How can one really discuss such chaos in concrete, logical terms, much less expect a well-reasoned conclusion?

MURAKAMI'S LANGUAGE: THE QUESTION OF PLAINSTYLE

One of the more interesting reviews to come out in the United States was that by Luc Sante (*New York Magazine*, Oct. 13, 1997), both for its on-the-mark estimation of the force that drives Murakami as a writer, and for its rather naive criticism of the translation of the work.

Sante points out, to begin with, that Murakami teases us with a series of facts and ideas, but probably does not himself understand fully the connections that hold them together. "He is writing you a letter—artless, urgent, perplexed—in which he tries to make sense of some odd events, giving you all the facts in proper order, hoping you will see the pattern that eludes him. This of course is a measure of just how devious he is." This is probably truer than Sante realizes, for Murakami, as I stated near the beginning of this book, has always seen writing as a process by which he himself may comprehend the events in his life and the society that surrounds him. As he writes hoping to enlighten his readers about their place in the world, he hopes equally to enlighten himself.

By and large, Sante's view of *The Wind-up Bird Chronicle* is positive; the work, like all literature, he says, "is not a tool or a code or a map but an object, period." Its potential, in other words, lies in what the reader makes of it.

He has harsher words on the subject of Rubin's translation of the work, which he describes as "slipshod," and in which he suspects elisions and even inaccuracy.

The dialogue in particular has all the rhythm and nuance of a hastily overdubbed foreign movie: "Look, I know how busy you are, but give me a break. I want to know what's going on. What's with the cat?" To come across such formulations in a novel not written by Franklin W. Dixon raises questions about how many shadings the translator might have flung overboard expeditiously, both there and in the less demotic passages.

I am not inclined to be very sympathetic to Sante's complaint here. As one who has read both the original and the translation of the novel carefully, as Sante obviously has not, I can detect no major flaws either in the idiom or in the tone of Rubin's rendering. What he has done, and quite effectively in my opinion, is to reproduce the flavor of Murakami's original brand of what might be termed "plainstyle," an intentionally simplified writing style popular among many contemporary writers in and outside of Japan. This style claims as one of its integral parts the very idiosyncracies noted by Sante in his review.

As part of his emphasis on using simple language, Murakami's writing comes across as neither polished, nor even especially neat. It lacks the subtlety that many associate with other major Japanese writers of this century, and this too is intentional. Perhaps more than any other writer alive in Japan today, Murakami rejects the idea of complex language as an art form, and focuses instead on getting his story across with as little distraction as possible. One thing Murakami *has* done with his language — and this is an achievement for Japanese writing as a whole — is to redefine its expression in ways that reflect the increasing influences on Japan of other languages and cultures around the world. His purpose in doing this is not to destroy the uniqueness of Japanese language and culture, but rather, as he told Jay McInerney in 1992, to bring Japanese culture — including its literature — into closer proximity with the rest of the world.

I think what young Japanese writers are doing is trying to reconstruct our language. We appreciate the beauty, the subtlety of the language Mishima used, but those days are gone. We should do something now. And what we are doing as contemporary writers is trying to break through the barrier of isolation so that we can talk to the rest of the world in our words again. (*New York Times Book Review*, Sep. 27, 1992)

In this regard Murakami and his contemporaries have been remarkably successful, and this has been picked up on by a great many scholars and critics around the world who remark on the seamlessness with which Murakami's prose seems to slide into other languages and cultural contexts. Rubin's translation of *The Wind-up Bird Chronicle* reflects Murakami's attempts to redefine his language, and while some will, like Sante, find it troubling and unsatisfactory, there is no denying that the plainstyle developed and employed by Murakami has achieved its objective: in ways that the works of Mishima and Tanizaki never could, it has helped to dispel much of the cloud of mystery that has shrouded popular perceptions of Japanese literature in the West since it began to be widely translated into English in the 1950s and 1960s.

CRITICAL RESPONSES IN JAPAN

Readers of Rubin's translation of *The Wind-up Bird Chronicle* actually have certain advantages over the Japanese readership of the original, published in monthly installments as *Nejimakidori Kuronikuru* between 1994 and 1995, for there was a significant gap between the release of the first two volumes of the work, which bound up all the serialized chapters, and the third volume, written by Murakami in response to widespread complaints that the novel was not really "finished."

There is justification for this complaint, though perhaps no more so than in any Japanese novel. The work does not, in fact, end with closure of the mystery; instead, it leaves us only with the sense that Toru himself is healing from the pain of having lost Kumiko.

Volume Two of *Nejimakidori Kuronikuru* ends like this: Toru swims in the neighborhood pool, and suddenly has a vision that he is in a gigantic well. Sunlight streams down to him, much as it did briefly on Mamiya in his own well, and Toru experiences a sense of well-being. He ends the novel accepting that he may or may not recover his wife, but at least he is prepared to deal with either eventuality.

Members of the literary community in Japan were sharply critical of this ending, feeling even more than critics of the translation that Murakami had let the mystery "get away from him." Murakami himself claims that he sincerely believed the novel finished at the end of Volume Two, and simply changed his mind in response to his readers' complaints. At the same time, he admits that while living abroad he began to move beyond the relatively passive stance that had marked his earlier writing, that a new sense of "activism" accounts for his desire to write a third volume. Thus, as the author engaged this new, more active stance, Toru Okada also became more militant. As Murakami stated while writing the third volume, "If I were the protagonist, I would *have* to get my wife back. I would want to fight" (Interview with Murakami).

He did not, however, initially tell his readers about this, and this led some to speculate, when the third volume was announced, that the author had been hoping to draw more readers into the mystery, to whet readers' appetites for more (presumably to increase sales). Whether we accept such an ungenerous analysis or not, it *does* seem to be true that Murakami hoped, originally, at least, that his readers would think about the ending of the second volume, and challenge themselves by drawing their own conclusions. "Originally I didn't tell anyone because I wanted the readers to finish it for themselves. I wanted them to decide for themselves what it all meant. If I had told them right away that Volume Three was on the way, no one would have bothered to think about it. By waiting, I forced them to use their heads a little. I made this public just last month, and some readers were angry about it!" (Interview with Murakami). At the same time, this reflects, perhaps, the interactive relationship Murakami seeks to establish with his readers. "*Nejima-kidori* was supposed to be a challenge to my readers," he claims. "At the end of Volume Two we are on the same ground. We have the same material. So Jay [Rubin] could write the next volume. So could you, just as well as I could. We are equal" (Interview with Murakami).

Unfortunately for Murakami, however, the addition of the third volume stirred up almost as much controversy as the initial decision to stop with the second one. Mitsuyoshi Numano, a critic writing

for the literary journal *Bungakukai*, was intrigued by the announce-
ment of a third volume and looked forward to its arrival (*Bungakukai*, Jul. 1994), but having read it a year later, thought the work
might as well have ended with Volume Two after all. "Even though
it leaves many of the mysterious unaccounted for, inasmuch as this
is how the real world is, I can't deny feeling that the novel might as
well have ended with Volume Two" (*Bungakukai*, Oct. 1995).

Other problems attended the addition of the new volume, most
important of which was the difficulty of making a transition from the
"ending" of Volume Two and the reopening of the narrative in Volume Three. A gap remains, one that was adroitly solved by Rubin,
who elected to remove the final scene of Toru in the swimming
pool, and end Book Two with Toru's attack on the man with the
guitar case. Thus, in some ways the translation of *The Wind-up Bird
Chronicle* actually functions more smoothly than did the original.

THE "DEFINITIVE" TEXT?

This leads me to one final issue, and this is the fact that *The Wind-
up Bird Chronicle* does, in fact, alter parts of the original. At least
one critic has expressed disappointment at this (Yoshiko Samuels
touches briefly on this in an article in *World Literature Today*), and
perhaps rightly.

It is worth noting that when Murakami approached Knopf with
his novel for possible publication in English, he was asked cut an
unspecified number of words (one unconfirmed report says 25,000,
the length of this book!). The author reportedly responded by making a series of excisions, but not enough to cut the book to the size
Knopf wanted. Rubin, then, fearing that the work would be carved
up by someone else, elected to make the excisions himself. His own

cuts in some cases take into account those of Murakami himself, but in other cases do not.

Most of these cuts do not especially alter our reading of the text, though not always. For instance, Chapter Thirty One of the hardcover edition of the original (about 150 pages from the end of Volume Three) contains a section in which Ushikawa tells Toru that "something critical" has been removed from Kumiko, and that this may be the result of a peculiar relationship between her and Noboru Wataya. Although Ushikawa will not go so far as to characterize this relationship as sexual, it certainly raises the possibility that Kumiko's problem stems from something similar to Creta Kano's.

Although alterations of this sort in the translation do raise issues about what constitutes the "definitive" text, we are also confronted by the fact that Murakami, having made the various excisions from his own text, ended up using many of these in the paperback edition of *Nejimakidori Kuronikuru* that was released in 1997. This means that not only is the translation of the text different from the original, but that there are significant differences between the hardcover and paperback editions as well. There are also "two" English translations: one in American English, the other with British spellings and expressions, released by Harvill. Add to this the fact that the work was initially released in monthly serialization, and we can only wonder, what *is* the "real" text? As Rubin noted in a round-table discussion with Philip Gabriel and Gary Fishketjon that appeared on the Knopf web page, "The more you look into [textual cuts] and into the question of revision, the more you realize that there is no single authoritative version of *any* Murakami work: he tinkers with everything long after it first finds its way into print." Defending his own revisions of the text in producing *The Wind-up Bird Chronicle*, Rubin suggests, however, that some day it may be necessary to

approach this issue again, perhaps followed by a new, more definitive translation.

An energetic graduate student could have a field day tracking down all
these differences, though it would probably be a waste of time. I do think,
though, that if *The Wind-up Bird Chronicle* outlives its time and becomes
part of the canon fifty years from now, a retranslation will be needed, and
scholars can have a fine time screaming about how Jay Rubin utterly
butchered the text. (Round-table discussion)

If all this tells us anything, it is that *The Wind-up Bird Chronicle*,
like so many Murakami works, must be viewed as much as a "work
in progress" as a finished text. This may account partially for the
fragmentary, unfinished feel we gain from the text. At the same
time, however, to return briefly to what I said earlier, Murakami
writes not so much to inform, but to explore for himself the problems of modern society, his own included. He does not pretend to
have the answers, but he certainly hopes to find some of them along
the way. And if he is unable to solve some of the mysteries that
emerge from his texts, this is surely because he does not know
himself. But this, too, is an important aspect of Murakami's realism.

4

The Novel's Performance

SALES IN JAPAN AND ABROAD

It can be said that Haruki Murakami's novels perform strongly, particularly during their first year. At the same time, excepting *Norwegian Wood* (1987), which sold two million copies in Japan, Murakami's sales tend to number in the hundreds of thousands. Even then, these figures are very strong, and indicate a loyal and growing readership. At this point in his career, Murakami could probably write anything and have it turn out a bestseller, if only because everyone wants to see what the latest Murakami book is all about.

The original Japanese publication of *The Wind-up Bird Chronicle* did at least as well, and in some cases better, than previous works. Because the work was released in three volumes in Japan it is impossible to give a precise figure for its sales there, but the first volume in hardcover went to twenty-six printings and sold roughly 344,000 copies; Volume Two made eleven printings and came in at approximately 276,000 copies, while the third volume sold about

237,000. All told, then, the work came appreciably close to selling a million copies combined. Paperback sales were even stronger: the three volumes sold approximately 453,000, 392,000, and 386,000 copies, respectively, totaling well over a million total copies.

Abroad, translations of Murakami's novels have also been respectable. In the United States his books tend to sell between five and fifteen thousand copies. His fiction has been translated into at least fourteen languages, and recently seems to be especially popular in Germany, Taiwan, and South Korea. *Norwegian Wood* was among the top forty bestselling books of 1998 in Korea, including fiction and nonfiction. In Taiwan, according to *Publisher's Weekly*, Murakami is *the* bestselling foreign author, and may be more popular even than in Japan.

The very bestselling translated author in Taiwan is the Japanese novelist Murakami Haruki. China Times has all of his books, five of which were among the 10 to China Times' credit on the Eslite Bookstore's top 100 sellers. "He is practically an industry here in Taiwan," says rights director Joyce Yen. "I think he is more popular here than in Japan." (Taylor, *Publisher's Weekly*, July 12, 1999)

This last may be questionable, but it is clear that in other industrialized Asian countries Murakami has found a ready following, and enjoys the status normally reserved for rock stars.

THE WIND-UP BIRD IN ENGLISH

In English *The Wind-up Bird Chronicle* seems to have done as well or better than many of the author's other translated works. While precise figures are difficult to come by, one reliable source suggests that as many as fourteen thousand copies of the hardcover edition were sold (compared with the estimate of just under seven thousand copies of *A Wild Sheep Chase* in hardcover, released by Kodansha). Whether sales of the paperback will do this well is difficult to say, but with Philip Gabriel's translation of *The Sputnik Sweetheart* now out, and the recent release of *Underground* in English (2000), there may be enough attention focused on Murakami to boost sales of his earlier works, too.

On the other hand, it is also true that *The Wind-up Bird Chronicle* did not perform in the same way some of the others discussed in this series did. For instance, there can be no question of Murakami's competing, in the English-language market, at least, with the *Harry Potter* books, whose regular appearance on all the major bestseller lists is phenomenal, or with Ondaatje's *The English Patient*, which turned into a major feature film. He does not yet have the kind of notoriety in the West that has made him Japan's top writer. While there may always be a small cult following of his works in, say, the United States or the United Kingdom, he will probably never be the "most talked-about" writer outside of his own country. More to the point, he may never be accepted as a *part* of the literary scene in the United States or United Kingdom, but will instead have to content himself with being a visitor to it—a celebrated visitor, no doubt—but still an outsider.

Why should this be? I am inclined to attribute the more modest inroads into the international market made by Murakami to his being perceived as a *Japanese* writer rather than a *world* writer. The distinction is admittedly a fine one, but it suggests the persistence of regional thinking that still marks much of our perception about writers and the worlds they describe. We are probably better able to think of a Hispanic writer, for instance, as "one of our own" than we are an Asian. (The same seems to be true in music; Ricky Martin, Gloria Estefan and Enrique Iglesias are part of the North American music scene, while Hikaru Utada and Ayumi Hamazaki

are "exotic"). This may be a matter of proximity, of habitual thinking concerning "the East" as opposed to "the West." It is interesting
to note, for instance, that another author in this series, Kazuo
Ishiguro, is often thought of as a "Japanese" author, despite the fact
that both he and his writing are unmistakably English. It seems to
be more a matter of his name, his ancestry, which places him into
the realm of "the East," by blood rather than culture, and occasionally causes confusion as to his "place" in world literature. Even
Murakami cannot resist pointing out that "There is a Japanese
personality in the English butler" in *Remains of the Day* (Wright,
Boston Magazine, Jan. 1994).

Murakami is, admittedly, a clearer case than Ishiguro, but I feel
that there *is* more resistance to reading a Japanese author as a world
author, or at least a hesitancy among mainstream English-speaking
readers to approach someone from the East. As a Japanese, his
worldview is (incorrectly!) assumed to be too exotic. We seem to
imagine a greater accessibility, say, to Gabriel Garcia-Marquez, or
Manuel Puig. This is not a case of discrimination so much as an
assumption regarding intelligibility that is grounded perhaps in the
still-dominant perception of Asia as something too alien for the
average Western reader to comprehend.

If this is why Murakami is not as widely read in the West as other
world writers, it is also one reason why many readers who *do* have a
look at his books are surprised by what they find. In fact, readers are
either turned on by the "normality" of the Murakami world (but
why should it *not* be normal . . . ?), or turned off by the same thing,
expecting a more exotic, "Japanese" flavor. One columnist for the
New York Times Book Review even complained that Murakami's
stories have *too* many Western cultural icons in them; he found it
disturbingly *un*Japanese that so many Murakami heroes ate Big
Macs and smoked Marlboros.

It is also true, of course, that Murakami's particular oeuvre as a writer is more rarefied than many others. He is, among other things, known as a writer of "magical realist" fiction, a seemingly oxymoronic term that describes realistic settings in which *anything* can happen—something like Laura Esquivel's *Like Water For Chocolate*, or Marquez's *One Hundred Years of Solitude*. This is entertainment reading, but it packs more punch, and demands more from the reader than the garden-variety novel.

As I suggested in the previous section, it is conceivable that *The Wind-up Bird Chronicle* will help to weaken some of the barriers encountered by Japanese fiction as it enters the English-speaking world. Murakami is often compared to major Western writers of his time—Thomas Pynchon, Raymond Carver, and so forth—and while the comparisons are not always favorable, it is a positive step that such comparisons can be made at all. Coming from the same culture that produced Mishima and Kawabata, writers with whom Western comparisons are often very difficult, Murakami has forced Western readers to reconsider their perceptions of what Japanese literature is or should be. In place of the "inscrutable oriental" image of Kawabata, Murakami shows us a literary establishment that is, at last, keeping pace with globalization, and representing major increases in the *bilateral* flow of cultural influence between East and West.

A good example of this bilateralism is the emergence of a young British writer, David Mitchell, who lives and writes in Hiroshima, and claims to have Murakami's works in his mind as he writes. Mitchell's latest novel, *number9dream* (Sceptre), bears the obvious imprint of Murakami's fictional world. Writing from the perspective of a Japanese protagonist, Eiji Miyake, Mitchell creates a character Murakami would recognize: hip, yet self-effacing, at once tough and timid, and positively driven by his longing for people who have disappeared from his life: his twin sister, who is dead; his mother, who is in an asylum; his father, whom he has never met, and now seeks in Tokyo. Like Murakami, Mitchell weaves a world that eases in and out of different modes of realities, and leaves us wondering— though usually not for long—whether the scene we have just read is really supposed to have happened, or if it was all just another of Eiji Miyake's fantasies.

Mitchell's case will probably not be the last, and we may expect other young writers to emerge in the future who, following Murakami's lead, will realize that Japanese culture is a living thing, something to be engaged and experimented with. In between the very English novels of Kazuo Ishiguro and the virtually Japanese novels of David Mitchell, Haruki Murakami seems to be standing in the middle, directing traffic. This must be very pleasing to Murakami, whose self-imposed exile beginning in 1986 showed him that knowledge of contemporary Japanese culture in the world is still very limited. As he commented in 1992,

I lived on a Greek island for a couple of years and although it was a very small island, everyone I talked to said "I drive a Nissan. It's a very good car." After a week I was tired of that, but I realized that Nissan, Casio, Seiko, Honda or Sony were the only Japanese words they knew. They knew nothing about Japanese culture, Japanese literature, Japanese music or anything like that. So I thought we have to do something to break through the isolation the Japanese have cherished for so long. (*New York Times Book Review*, Sep. 27, 1992)

Murakami's fiction offers Western readers a view of Japan that demystifies its exotic nature, and this is a positive step. At the same time, he is internationally sophisticated enough to show us a thing or two about ourselves. As Jamie James writes, "In Murakami's early books, the references to Western pop culture were sometimes so obscure that they even flew over the heads of many Americans" (James, *New York Times Book Review*, Nov. 2, 1997). This may be true, though I suspect that most of these cases involved younger readers encountering the icons of the 1950s and 1960s — Murakami's past, but also part of the global cultural movements of those decades. In this way Murakami invites Western readers his own age to look back at their own lives, while giving younger readers a window into the culture of their parents.

In short, Murakami has pioneered a strain of Japanese literature that is potentially as revealing to Westerners — particularly Americans — about their own culture as it is to Japanese readers about theirs. At the same time, Kenzaburo Oe's earlier comment notwithstanding, this *is* Japanese literature; it is literature that takes into account the radical changes in Japan's surface, popular culture, and permits discerning readers a glimpse of how such influences have meshed with a more traditional one. The reason Murakami has done so well both in and out of Japan is the fact that he has brought Japan up to date, offering an alternative picture of Japanese culture that shows how one can affect foreign cultural icons — Levi's, Budweiser beer, The Beatles — and still be "Japanese."

In this sense, *The Wind-up Bird Chronicle* may not have started any major trends, but it is part of a major trend, one that forces Japanese and non-Japanese alike to confront the changing shape of "national culture," perhaps even to accept that, as cultural boundaries constantly shift, the idea of an insular, homogenized, "native" culture becomes obsolete.

5

Further Reading and Discussion Questions

SUGGESTIONS FOR ADDITIONAL READING

Readers of Haruki Murakami are fortunate in that they enjoy a large body of compatriots around the world. There are many sites on the Internet where they may seek additional information, comments from other readers, informative articles, and occasionally even responses from Murakami himself. In addition to the fact that this remarkable medium exists, Murakami is one writer who has proved his willingness to be available to readers for questions and comments. Up until a few years ago he even maintained a web site to which readers could send their comments and questions, and whenever possible he took the trouble to answer them on-line. Eventually this proved too much even for the energetic Murakami, however, and he settled for publishing a collection of the most representative questions, along with his responses, in book form. Regrettably, the book currently exists only in Japanese.

In terms of the author's works themselves, most are available in English translation. Notable works include those mentioned in the text above: *A Wild Sheep Chase*, translated by Alfred Birnbaum, was released by Kodansha and later by Plume; *Hard-Boiled Wonderland and the End of the World*, also translated by Birnbaum, is another worthwhile read. Those interested in the author's short stories are encouraged to seek out *The Elephant Vanishes*, translated by Birnbaum and Jay Rubin, released by Knopf. Many of these short works have also been released in literary magazines in the United States—especially *The New Yorker*—but readers will probably find it easier and more convenient just to locate the book.

More recently, Rubin and Philip Gabriel have been busy translating Murakami's new books almost as fast as he can write them. Rubin's rendering of *Norwegian Wood*, the author's 1987 blockbuster, will be out by the time this book goes to press, and preliminary reviews are very positive. Gabriel's most recent contribution is *The Sputnik Sweetheart* (originally published in 1999), released by Harvill in May, 2001. Gabriel and Birnbaum have also collaborated to bring out a translation of *Underground*, Murakami's most important nonfiction work to date, containing interviews with victims and perpetrators of the infamous 1995 sarin gas incident in the Tokyo subways.

Among secondary literature—works *about* Murakami—readers will find the list shorter, but material is available. *Japan Quarterly*, available in many libraries, has printed articles by Rubin (Oct.-Dec. 1992), Glynne Waley (Jan.-March, 1997), and myself (Jan.-Mar. 1998). In addition to these, Rubin's review of *A Wild Sheep Chase* in *The World & I* (April 1990), if it can still be found, contains an excellent introduction to Murakami literature in general.

Two other, more academically-oriented essays of my own have appeared in *The Journal of Asian Studies* (May, 1998) and *The Journal of Japanese Studies* (Summer, 1999). These should be available in many university libraries, and contain more detailed explications of some of the theories mentioned only briefly in the present text—notably, my theory of the "nostalgic image," and Murakami's use of "magical realism."

In book form, readers will find Stephen Snyder's brilliant reading of *Hard-Boiled Wonderland and the End of the World* enlightening, included in a collection of essays entitled *In Pursuit of Contemporary East Asian Culture* (Westview Press). There is also a useful chapter on Murakami in Susan Napier's acclaimed study, *The Fantastic in Modern Japanese Literature: The Subversion of Modernity* (Routledge). Finally, my own book, entitled *Dances with Sheep: The Quest for Identity in the Fiction of Murakami Haruki*, contains detailed analyses of all the author's major works, and will be out well in advance of the present text as part of the Center for Japanese Studies Monograph Series at the University of Michigan.

DISCUSSION ISSUES

Numerous questions deserving greater detail than I could offer above suggested themselves as this book unfolded. These are issues and problems that I hope will make useful material for discussion on the internet or in further writing.

The first of these is, of course, what are some alternative readings for the "wind-up bird?" I have offered one reading, but as I said, the bird, like the sheep in *A Wild Sheep Chase*, is an "open" symbol, meaning that it can and should be interpreted in different ways, depending on what one is getting out of the rest of the text. Is the bird "fate," or perhaps just a bad luck charm? Is it possible to read it in a more positive light? Toru offers two possible interpretations—one in which the bird "winds the springs of the world," and another in which it presages doom. Which reading is more accurate?

Another worthwhile issue, one for which there was insufficient space in the main text, is the role Cinnamon really plays in this story. On the surface of things he guides Toru closer to his solution, but it seems equally possible to read him as a kind of omniscient force responsible for creating *all* the events in the story. Support for such a reading lies in Toru's descriptions of Cinnamon's computer, a labrynthine structure that cannot fail to remind us of the "hotel" that constitutes Toru's inner mind. Is it not possible, then, to imagine that *everything* that happens to Toru is really part of an imaginary structure constructed by Cinnamon with his computer? Fans of Larry and Andy Wachowski's feature film *The Matrix* may find this question appealing.

Also worth exploring is the identity of some of the less-encountered characters in the story. At the top of my list is the "man without a face" in the unconscious hotel. Who is this man? The fact that he *knows* the labyrinth of the hotel corridors, yet does not have complete knowledge of the whole structure, might lead us to associate him with Cinnamon, come to assist Toru through the maze. But we also recall that when asked his identity, he replies only that he is "the hollow man," a remark that seems more suited to Mamiya, another sympathetic character. One might even manage to read him as Toru himself, opening the possibility of a *third* structure within the self. This question is particularly interesting in that how we choose to answer it may affect our overall reading of the book.

The matter of Noboru's actual purpose is also a major question, all the more interesting for us as readers because it is never really solved. All we really have is Toru's own speculation: " 'Now he is trying to bring out something that the great mass of people keep hidden in the darkness of their unconscious. He wants to use it for his own political advantage . . . it's directly connected to the darkest depths of history, because its final effect is to destroy and obliterate people on a massive scale' " (583). What, we might ask, is the "political advantage" Noboru seeks in drawing the core identity out of the "great mass of people"? The mass media is portrayed as an accomplice in this, much as it is in *A Wild Sheep Chase*, and it would be interesting to explore Murakami's depictions of the media, in this and other novels as well.

Connected with the mass media is the State itself, under heavy scrutiny as it has been in many Murakami novels since the early 1980s. In *Hard-Boiled Wonderland and the End of the World* the State is not only depicted as sinister and virtually all powerful; in the undeclared "war" over information and technology in that work, it plays *both sides of the conflict*, using unsuspecting people as bait to gain access to the information it seeks to control. The appearance of the Japanese State is more subtle in *The Wind-up Bird Chronicle*, references reduced generally to the movements of Noboru himself, but we *do* always sense its existence, even if we are a little unclear on its ultimate role in the narrative.

More general issues include the structure of the novel: how, for instance, do the narratives concerning Japan's past history impact on the present narrative of Toru and Kumiko? Toru provides a fairly straightforward progression of connections between the events of the past and those in his own life on pages 501–502 as follows:

These "clients" and I were joined by the mark on my cheek. Cinnamon's grandfather (Nutmeg's father) and I were also joined by the mark on my cheek. Cinnamon's grandfather and Lieutenant Mamiya were joined by the city of Hsin-ching. Lieutenant Mamiya and the clairvoyant Mr. Honda were joined by their special duties on the Manchurian-Mongolian border, and Kumiko and I had been introduced to Mr. Honda by Noboru Wataya's family. Lieutenant Mamiya and I were joined by our experiences in our respective wells — his in Mongolia, mine on the property where I was sitting now. Also on this property had once lived an army officer who had commanded troops in China. All of these were linked as in a circle, at the center of which stood prewar Manchuria, continental East Asia, and the short war of 1939 in Nomonhan.

All of this is true, and an interesting analysis of the novel *could* begin with this list of connections, sifting through the various layers of truth, of probable fabrication (particularly the stories Cinnamon tells), of magic and reality, past and present. How might our analysis change, for instance, if we eliminate whatever is only *probable*, or if we reject anything "magical" as impossible? And finally, if we conclude (as, ultimately, I think we must) that the magical and the fabricated must play a role in this novel at least as much as things we consider beyond doubt, what does this say about the literary world of Haruki Murakami as a whole, or about his worldview as a writer?

This takes us to the difficult concept of the "postmodern." I have been reluctant to approach this topic at all in this volume, chiefly because it takes us into areas of theoretical contentiousness that will only muddy the waters. But for those who have encountered the term before, who know a little of its murky history and the debates that continue to surround its character, a "postmodern" analysis of this novel would yield a great deal. Such analyses would focus on defending the coexistence of realism and the magical, on the nature of historical "fact" and historical "conjecture," and might even suggest that the "histories" provided in the novel—particularly those concerning the war—have as much validity as conventional historical writings of that period. However, determined as I am *not* to create new problems so close to the end of this book, and since this subject is covered in some detail in my other writings, I will leave the matter here!

FOR READERS OF OTHER MURAKAMI WORKS

Finally, for readers of other Murakami fiction, I would like to suggest a few general questions that may be applied to *The Wind-up Bird Chronicle*, but are equally applicable to other works. These, hopefully, will allow further crossreading between the various major works in translation.

First is the matter of names. From the obviously silly instances like "Noboru Wataya/Mackerel the cat" to the merely bizarre, such as Cinnamon and Nutmeg Akasaka, names have always been treated oddly in Murakami fiction. Many characters have no names; others are named by some other character. A deeper exploration of how names are used, not used, or abused, would be interesting.

A second question concerns entrances and exits. Murakami is very big on the relationship between entrances and exits. In *Pinball, 1973* (regrettably one of the few works not available in English outside of Japan) he writes as follows:

Wherever there is an entrance there is also an exit. Most things are built that way: mailboxes, electric vacuum cleaners, zoos, turkey basters. Of course, there are also things that are not built that way. Mouse traps, for instance. (*Murakami Haruki Zensakuhin 1979–1989*, 1:129)

As the above suggests, that which contains an entrance but not an exit is a trap. A similar situation faces the protagonist of *Hard-Boiled Wonderland and the End of the World*, whose escape route from his inner mind is gradually closing, leaving him with no exit back to the conscious world. The idea turns up in *The Sputnik Sweetheart*, as well, when a beautiful young pianist is trapped on a Ferris wheel, the door locked from outside, and therein encounters a vision that changes her life. Later in the book, her young companion disappears into some mysterious world, presumably by magic, from which there is no apparent way out.

Readers will have noticed a similar theme in *The Wind-up Bird Chronicle*, too: alleys blocked at both ends (with obvious symbolic implications); a labrynthine unconscious hotel from which there does not *seem* to be a locatable exit; deep wells whose exits are more difficult to access than their entrances; Kumiko's inescapable "prison."

Stories themselves, according to Murakami, can be like this. Every narrative is potentially a labyrinth, and the writer faces the danger of becoming entangled with each new story.

What does this obsession on becoming trapped mean to Murakami and his characters? Who entraps them, and why? As one of the major themes running throughout Murakami fiction, this question could be discussed in a variety of ways.

Finally, and perhaps most important of all, is the theme of loss. Murakami protagonists are always losing things—friends, objects, lovers, their youth, their idealism. Indeed, it is almost heartbreaking to watch the protagonists of the author's early works desperately searching for the things they have lost, only to find that there is no hope of recovering the past.

This in mind, it would be interesting to examine the various losses suffered by Murakami's protagonists in greater detail, to compare his early works with more recent ones. How, for instance, does Toru Watanabe in *Norwegian Wood* handle the loss of someone he loves as compared with Toru Okada in *The Wind-up Bird Chronicle*? What steps does the protagonist of *A Wild Sheep Chase* take to recover his best friend Rat when he believes him to be threatened? Have Murakami's heroes become more militant, as I suggested earlier? These questions deserve further attention.

SOME USEFUL DISCUSSION FORUMS AND INTERNET SITES

It is my hope that these questions will be of use to readers, and that many more will be discussed by interested readers on-line in the coming months. Below I would like to list a few of the forums on-line that exist for such discussions, realizing, however, that by the time this book is in print some of them may no longer exist.

http://www.shimonoseki-cu.ac.jp/~uekura/haruki/

Contains a list of Murakami's works in English translation and where to find them (up to 1999).

http://www.geocities.com/Paris/3954/haruki.htm

"The World of Murakami Haruki" by Amy Tak-yee Lai of the Faculty of English, University of Cambridge. Contains a reader's forum and links to several articles and reviews of the author's works, as well as other web pages on Murakami.

http://www.kyoto-su.ac.jp/information/famous/murakamih.html

A site by Maiko Hisada containing a brief biographical sketch of Murakami.

http://www.anotherscene.com/japanpm/murakami.html

Part of a site by Earl Jackson dedicated to "postmodern Japan." This page, though a little dated (does not include recent release of *Norwegian Wood* in the United States and United Kingdom), contains very useful links to reviews and commentaries on the author's various works (some links are "dead" at this time, however).

http://www.asahi-net.or.jp/~hf2t-skym/neji/bibliography/
1.html

A list of translations of the author's works, and more importantly, of secondary sources. The site was last updated in 1998, however, and does not contain some of the more recent critical work on the subject.

http://haruki.homestead.com/Links.html

One of the best sites on Murakami, this one is very up-to-date in terms of its list of translated works out there, and contains articles, commentaries, and links to reviews of the author's works. *Definitely* a good place to visit.

There are other sites out there, mostly containing reviews and short essays on the author that readers are encouraged to seek out. Most regrettable among this list is the loss of the "Murakami Haruki Asahi-do," a website maintained for some years by the *Asahi Shimbun* in Japan. For the time being, at any rate, it appears to be closed.

Good luck, and happy hunting!

BIBLIOGRAPHY

I. Works by Haruki Murakami

1973-nen no pinbōru (Pinball, 1973). In *Murakami Haruki Zensakuhin, 1979–1989*, Vol. 1. Originally published by Kōdansha, 1980.
Andāguraundo (Underground). Tokyo: Kōdansha, 1997.
A Wild Sheep Chase. Translated by Alfred Birnbaum. New York: Plume, 1989.
Dance Dance Dance. Translated by Alfred Birnbaum. Tokyo & New York: Kodansha International, 1994.
The Elephant Vanishes. Translated by Alfred Birnbaum and Jay Rubin. New York: Knopf, 1993.

Hard-Boiled Wonderland and the End of the World. Translated by Alfred Birnbaum. New York: Vintage, 1991.

Kaze no uta o kike (Hear the wind sing). In *Murakami Haruki Zensakuhin, 1979–1989*, Vol. 1. Originally published by Kōdansha, 1979.

Murakami Haruki Zensakuhin, 1979–1989 (Complete works of Haruki Murakami, 1979–1989). 8 volumes. Tokyo: Kōdansha, 1990–1991.

Nejimakidori kuronikuru (Wind-up bird chronicle). Tokyo: Shinchōsha, 1994–1996.

Norwegian Wood. Translated by Jay Rubin. New York: Vintage, 2000.

South of the Border, West of the Sun. Translated by Philip Gabriel. New York: Knopf, 1999.

The Sputnik Sweetheart. Translated by Philip Gabriel. London: Harvill, 2001.

Underground. Translated by Alfred Birnbaum and Philip Gabriel. New York: Vintage International, 2001.

The Wind-up Bird Chronicle. Translated by Jay Rubin. New York: Knopf, 1997.

Yakusoku sareta basho de: Underground 2 (At the place that was promised: Underground 2). Tokyo: Bungei Shunjū.

Miscellaneous

Interview with Haruki Murakami conducted by the author, October 22, 1994, in Cambridge, Massachussetts.

II. Select Criticism and Reviews

Buruma, Ian. "Turning Japanese." In *The New Yorker* (Dec. 23 & 30, 1996). 60–71.

James, Jamie. "East Meets West." In *The New York Times Book Review* (November 2, 1997).

Kakutani, Michiko. " 'The Wind-up Bird Chronicle': A Nightmarish Trek Through History's Web." In *The New York Times Book Review* (October 31, 1997).

Kawamoto, Saburō. " 'Monogatari' no tame no bōken" (A wild "story" chase). Interview with Murakami Haruki. In *Bungakukai* 39:8 (August 1985). 34–86.

Mathew, David. "On *The Wind-up Bird Chronicle*—Fiction from a Rising Son." Book review on-line (http://www.iplus.zetnet.co.uk).

Miller, Laura. "The Wind-up Bird Chronicle." Book review. In *Salon* (November 24, 1997).

Mitchell, David. *number9dream*. London: Sceptre (2001).

Mitgang, Herbert. (Review of *The Elephant Vanishes*) "From Japan, Big Macs and Marlboros in Stories." In *The New York Times Book Review* (May 12, 1993).

Murakami, Haruki. With Kawai Hayao. " 'Monogatari' de ningen wa nani o naosu no ka?" (What can humans cure with "stories"?). In *Sekai* 46: 621 (April 1996). 256–280.

———. With Jay McInerney. "Roll Over Basho: Who Japan Is Reading, and Why." In *The New York Times Book Review* (September 27, 1992).

Napier, Susan. *The Fantastic in Modern Japanese Literature: The Subversion of Modernity*. London: Routledge, 1996.

Numano, Mitsuyoshi. "Murakami Haruki wa sekai no 'ima' ni tachimukau" (Murakami Haruki faces the "now" of the world). In *Bungakukai* (July 1994). 156–164.

———. With Suzumura Kazunari. " 'Nejimakidori' wa doko e tobu ka?" (To where will the "wind-up bird" fly?). In *Bungakukai* (October 1995). 100–123.

Oe, Kenzaburo with Kazuo Ishiguro. "The Novelist in Today's World: A Conversation." In *Japan in the World*. Edited by Masao Miyoshi and H. D. Harootunian. Durham and London: Duke University Press, 1993. 163–176.

———. "Japan's Dual Identity: A Writer's Dilemma." In *Postmodernism and Japan*. Edited by Masao Miyoshi and H. D. Harootunian. Durham and London: Duke University Press, 1989. 189–213.

Rao, Kavitha, and Murakami, Mitsuko. "The Human Cost." In *Asiaweek* (October 3, 1997).

Rubin, Jay. "Deep Sheep Dip." Book review. In *The World & I* (April 1990). 384–390.

———. With Gary Fisketjon and Philip Gabriel. Roundtable discussion. See website at http://www.aaknopf.com.

———. "The Other World of Murakami Haruki." In *Japan Quarterly* (October-December 1992). 490–501.

Sante, Luc. "Oddville." Book review. In *New York Magazine* (October 13, 1997).

Snyder, Stephen. "Two Murakamis and Marcel Proust: Memory as Form in Contemporary Japanese Fiction." In *In Pursuit of Contemporary East Asian Culture*. Edited by Xiaobing Tang and Stephen Snyder. Boulder: Westview Press, 1996. 69–83.

Stalph, Jürgen. "Doitsu no Murakami Haruki" (Haruki Murakami and Germany). In *Kokubungaku*. 40:4 (March 1995). 104–108.

Strecher, Matthew. "Beyond 'Pure' Literature: Mimesis, Formula, and the Postmodern in the Fiction of Murakami Haruki." In *The Journal of Asian Studies* 57:2 (May 1998). 354–378.

———. *Dances With Sheep: The Quest for Identity in the Fiction of Murakami Haruki*. Ann Arbor: University of Michigan Press, 2001.

———. "Magical Realism and the Search for Identity in the Fiction of Murakami Haruki." In *Journal of Japanese Studies* 25:2 (Summer 1999). 263–298.

———. "Murakami Haruki: Japan's Coolest Writer Heats Up." In *Japan Quarterly* (January-March 1998). 61–69.

Taylor, Sally. "Books in Taiwan—Still Flourishing." In *Publisher's Weekly* (July 12, 1999).

Walley, Glynne. "Two Murakamis and their American influence." In *Japan Quarterly* (January-March 1997). 41–51.

Wright, Sarah. "Dancing as Fast as He Can." In *Boston Magazine* (January, 1994).